COPYRIGHT NOTICE

PREFACE

The goal of this book is to give a basic understanding of a fire alarm system. It was written with the goal of orientating, not just someone with basic electrical installation experience, but also someone with no experience in any trade. The topics covered in this book include:

- The basic types of fire alarm systems and how the latter integrates with other systems.
- The components that make up the fire alarm system.
- Wiring diagrams describing how the fire alarm devices work.
- Wiring and installation methods as per the National Electrical Code®.
- Fire alarm floor plans, riser diagrams and matrix of operations.

Throughout this book we will present information from the National Electrical Code® (NFPA 70®) 2014 version and NFPA 72® 2016 version. The National Electrical Code® sets the foundation for electrical safety in residential, commercial, and industrial occupancies. The NEC® contains the minimum requirements for installing electrical equipment; including fire alarm systems. When conduit is installed, the NEC® shall be consulted to determine mounting requirements. The NFPA® 72 specifies the application, installation, location, performance, inspection, testing, and maintenance of fire alarm systems. For example, NFPA 72® allows an installer to determine how many alarm notification appliances are required for a particularly sized room. The International Building Code®, in contrast, generally describes which occupancies (buildings) require a fire alarm system and which type of system. For example, to determine which type of fire alarm system would be required for a 30-story hotel, International Building Code® shall be consulted. As a future fire alarm installer/technician, you should familiarize yourself with both NEC® and NFPA 72®. Normally, International Building Code® is used by engineers and system designers.

It shall be noted that usually, codes and standards, as those found in NEC® and NFPA 72®, will be amended by local authorities. Changes or amendments are made to fit requirements or intent of the authority applying such codes and standards.

Starting from chapter 2, the reader will be presented with questions focused on the theory that was presented. The reader should make every effort to complete each question. For answer to the questions, please email the author below.

Various reviews were made to the grammar, spelling and correctness of the terms in this book. If you, the reader, believe that an error has been made, please send an email to the author: website@firealarmscertified.com

NFPA 72® and National Fire Alarm and Signaling Code ® are registered trademarks of the National Fire Protection Association, Quincy, MA.

ABOUT THE AUTHOR

 Henry Nazar P.E. is a former supervising electrical and fire alarm inspector with The Fire Department of New York. Mr. Nazar is a registered Professional Engineer in the State of New York. Henry Nazar has a Bachelor of Electrical Engineering Degree (B.E.E.) from The City College of New York.

Mr. Nazar has over 10 years of experience in teaching electrical and fire alarm installations in various trade schools. In 2016, Mr. Nazar started working with The Fire Department of New York as an electrical/fire alarm inspector where he inspected various fire alarm installations ranging from high-rise voice systems, auxiliary radio communications systems (ARCS), fire pumps and dual-fire command station setups. Mr. Nazar serves as a member in The NYC Department of Buildings Electrical Code Committee for Fire Pumps and Fire Alarm Systems (NEC Articles 695 and 760).

Henry Nazar is currently a fire protection consultant and designer in New York. He is the president of Nazar Engineering P.C. To contact Henry Nazar about consulting, designing, or pre-inspection of fire alarm systems or ARCS use the following email address: Nazar@NazarEngineering.Com.

TABLE OF CONTENTS

Chapter 1

OBJECTIVES:

➢ Understand the purpose of the fire alarm system.

➢ Understand how the fire alarm system integrates with building system functions.

➢ Discuss the design process of the fire alarm system as well as the installation phase and maintenance.

➢ Discuss the two basic types of fire alarm systems.

Introduction

The main purpose of the fire alarm system is to detect the presence of fire via various means, and on most occasions, notify building occupants or notify the central station monitoring the fire alarm system. In other words, the main purpose of the fire alarm system is to protect occupants and property from a fire. There are different means as to which a fire alarm system detects the presence of a fire. In this book, we will discuss the most widely used methods.

Fire Alarm System used for releasing Fire Extinguishing Agent

FIGURE 1

Most fire alarm systems installed are provided for life safety purposes. Their main function is to protect the lives of the building occupants. The system accomplishes this via various fire detection methods. One method of detection is via smoke detectors. As per the writing of this book, 50–80% of fire deaths are the result of smoke inhalation injuries, including burns to the respiratory system. It is crucial for the fire alarm system to be in proper working order, to detect the presence of smoke, activate the appropriate output functions (i.e. horns and strobes), so that it can accomplish its goal in alerting building occupants to evacuate the premises.

Other goals of a fire alarm system include the protection of property. One example is a fire suppression system for a computer server room. The fire alarm system would be used to activate the release of the agent used to extinguish the fire within the room. A clean agent, such as FM200, can be used to starve the room or fire of oxygen and not cause damage to the computer equipment.

Fire Alarm System and Integration with Other Building Systems

Since the fire alarm system is used, on most occasions, to provide life safety protection, the system must integrate with other systems of a building. These include:

- HVAC equipment – As per Building Code, the fire alarm system must shut down air handling units above 2,000 CFMs. This is accomplished via modules or relays connected from the Fire Alarm Control Unit to the HVAC unit or other control points.
- Door release equipment – Building code and NFPA 72® require that any electrically held exit door be unlocked upon activation of an alarm condition.
- Elevator recall – Building code requires that building elevators recall upon activation of an associated alarm condition. Again, this is accomplished by connecting the fire alarm system, via modules and relays, to the elevator controller.
- Music shut-down – Though not a general requirement as described above, music shutdown is many times designed by the engineer to meet the decibel level requirements described in NFPA 72®.

FIGURE 2

Figure 2 shows one common way the fire alarm system can integrate with HVAC equipment. Upon detection of an alarm condition, the fire alarm control unit will activate the relay (pictured) and shut-down the air handling unit. Shutting down fans that supply air into the premises is crucial during a fire. Feeding oxygen into a fire can cause the fire to burn much more quickly and easily, potentially causing fires to burn out of control. In addition, air handling units can transfer smoke from one area of a building to another; making it difficult for firefighters to contain and control the fire and putting occupants on other areas or floors at risk.

In later chapters we will discuss the various components that make up a fire alarm system.

Design, Installation and Maintenance of the Fire Alarm System

The installation of a fire alarm system typically starts with the design process. An engineering company will design the fire alarm plans using the building layout, and using applicable codes, draft the devices and necessary equipment on the plans. Many jurisdictions have strict requirements as to whom is allowed to design a fire alarm system; for examples, in New York City (5 boroughs), only a New York State licensed Professional Engineer (or Registered Architect) is allowed to design a fire alarm system. Other jurisdictions allow a NICET Level IV professional as well as a licensed professional engineer.

After the design phase has been completed, the installation of the system can begin. Technicians and installers use the plans created by the designer to determine the location of the devices to be installed as well as the type of fire alarm system that will be used (temporal-3 fire alarm system, voice communication system). In New York City, only a licensed master electrician is permitted (by local law) to install the fire alarm system and all necessary equipment such as conduits, boxes and cables. Following the installation, a licensed fire alarm installer (licensed by New York State) is permitted to "program" the fire alarm system. It should be noted that many jurisdictions strictly prohibit the installation of a fire alarm system without first obtaining approval from the authority having jurisdiction (building department or fire department).

After the installation has been completed, the system owner (usually the building owner) will schedule for an inspection with the authority having jurisdiction (AHJ). In NYC, the AHJ is the Fire Department of New York. An official inspection would be conducted by testing of the entire system. A letter of approval will be generated at the end of the inspection after all defects have been rectified.

Though the fire alarm system has gone through a plan review process and inspections as described above, after final sign off by the AHJ, the system must be maintained by a contracted company. The maintenance will ensure the system is functioning as it should and that any issues can be rectified.

Basic Types of Fire Alarm Systems

Though there are many different types of fire alarm systems, in this book, we will concentrate on the most widely used as this is the types you, the student, will encounter in the field.

Protected Premises (Local) Fire Alarm System

NFPA 72® defines a protected premises (local) fire alarm system as a system that consists of components and circuits arranged to monitor and annunciate the status of fire alarm or supervisory signal-initiating devices and to initiate the appropriate response to those signals, located at the protected premises. An example of such a system is a fire alarm system consisting of smoke detectors, manual pull stations, horns and strobes at a bank or retail store. When a smoke detector is activated, the fire alarm system will initiate an evacuation of the protected premises by activating the horns and strobes.

Figure 3 is an example of a protected premises (local) fire alarm system installed at a local medical office. Monitoring of a fire is done via the smoke detector. In the event of a fire, the

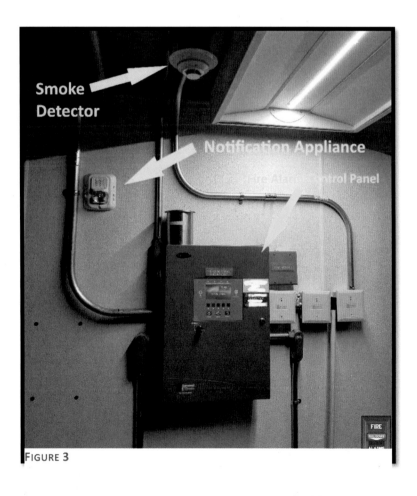

FIGURE 3

smoke detector will annunciate its condition at the Fire Alarm Control Unit. The appropriate response for this system is to activate the notification appliances (horn/strobe).

The protected premises fire alarm system integrates with other systems in order to accomplish its goal. Such systems include: Fan shut-down by connecting to the HVAC system, Door release by connecting to security systems, elevator recall functions by connecting to the elevator control circuitry.

In-Building Fire Emergency Voice/Alarm Communications System

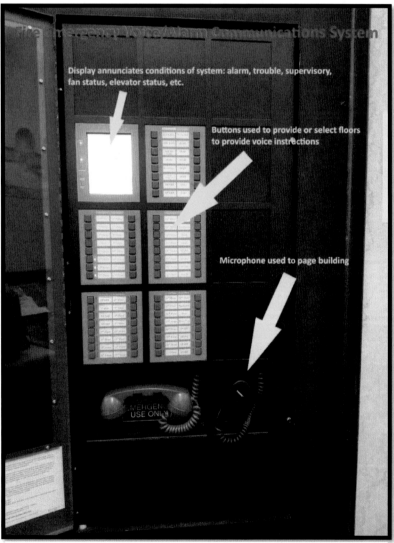

Fire Emergency Voice/Alarm Communications System

Display annunciates conditions of system: alarm, trouble, supervisory, fan status, elevator status, etc.

Buttons used to provide or select floors to provide voice instructions

Microphone used to page building

EMERGENCY USE ONLY

FIGURE 4

As per NFPA 72® definition, this system is defined as a dedicated manual or automatic equipment for originating and distributing voice instructions, as well as alert and evacuation signals pertaining to a fire emergency, to the occupants of a building. This system consists of a fire alarm system which has the capability to page or provide voice instructions to the building occupants in the event of a fire condition. The fire alarm system accomplishes this by using amplifiers, speakers and a microphone. The system has the capability to page on a floor by floor basis, or provide an "all-call" message to all building occupants. These systems are mostly required in high-rise buildings (greater than 75 feet to the highest occupied floor), as well as some large sized buildings, places of assembly (church, theater) when the occupant load exceeds a certain value. Figure 4 is an example of a Fire Alarm Control Unit with Voice Communications used in a high-rise office building in NYC. Fire Emergency Voice/Alarm Communications systems have the capability to provide voice instructions on a floor-by-floor basis by simply enabling the floor button, or various floors by selection of various buttons. A separate button is provided for "all-call" which enables all speakers to provide voice instructions to all building occupants. In later chapters, we will describe the speakers used with this system.

Building codes require that the voice communication control panel be installed nearest the entrance of the building, to allow responding personnel access to it once they arrive at the premises. NFPA 72® requires that controls be located or secured to allow access only by trained and authorized personnel. This is usually accomplished by providing a certain type of key access to the control panel. This key is a standard key used by emergency responding personnel (fire department). NFPA 72® also requires that controls be clearly identified. Labels are placed adjacent to the control buttons on the control panel.

There are various other types of fire alarm systems described in NFPA 72®. We have chosen not to include them in this publication. As an installer, most of your time will be spent on the two types of systems described above.

Chapter 2

OBJECTIVES:

➢ Understand the basic components that make up a Fire Alarm System.

➢ Discuss the functions of the fire alarm control unit.

➢ Describe the initiating device circuit and the devices that connect to it.

➢ Describe the notification appliances and how they work.

➢ Discuss the difference between a conventional-zoned fire alarm system and an addressable fire alarm system.

We will discuss in this chapter the system components that make up a fire alarm system. We will discuss the function of the fire alarm control unit, the remote annunciator, initiating devices (supervisory and alarm), and notification appliances.

Fire Alarm Control Unit

The fire alarm control unit, also known as the fire alarm control panel, is the brains of the entire

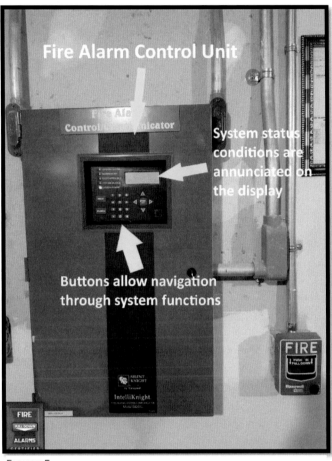

FIGURE 5

system. The control unit provides the interconnection of all the fire alarm devices: it provides the "input" connections from the field initiating devices (smoke detectors, pull stations, pressure switches, tamper switches), and the "output" power to the notification appliances (strobes, horns, bells) as well as the connection to other building functions. The Fire Alarm Control Unit is usually connected to 120 VAC power; this power or voltage is then, generally, dropped or transformed to 12VDC or 24VDC for the field devices. The Fire Alarm Control Unit also provides system information such as alarm conditions, and supervisory or trouble conditions. This information is generally graphically displayed on the LCD screen or, for a conventional-zoned system, is displayed using labeled LED indicators.

Functions that are controlled at the fire alarm control unit include: restarting of building air-handling units that have been shut down by the fire alarm system during an alarm condition, silencing of the outputs or notification appliance circuits, releasing of any electrically held doors, as well as other features.

FIGURE 6

The fire alarm control unit is usually installed in the main entrance of the building, if not, then a remote annunciator must be provided nearest the entrance for responding personnel. Figure 6 shows a fire alarm remote annunciator installed in a low-rise residential apartment building. The fire alarm control unit was installed in the cellar of the building, therefore a remote annunciator is provided at the main entrance to facilitate an efficient response to the situation. NFPA 72® requires that a remote annunciator be readily accessible and be properly identified as such. Usually a placard is provided by the installer adjacent to the remote annunciator identifying it as such.

Initiating Devices

Initiating devices are input devices that are connected to the Fire Alarm Control Unit's (conventional zoned system) Initiating Device Circuit (IDC) terminals. Devices that connect to this circuit send an input signal to the fire alarm control unit by closing a set of contacts when the device is actuated (ex: smoke detector, manual pull station). Control units with IDCs are known as conventional systems or zoned systems; there is no programming involved in the devices, all devices connected to a single initiating device circuit are known as a zone. If three smoke detectors are connected to a single IDC or zone, the fire alarm control unit cannot identify the location of the smoke detector, or which specific smoke detector actuated, it can only display the zone.

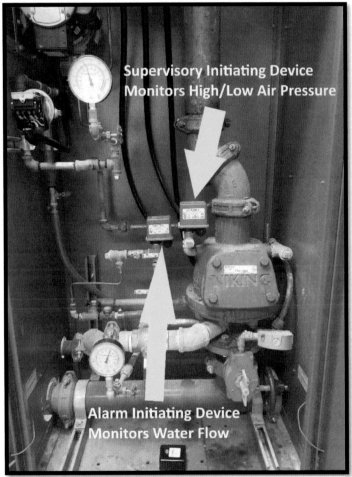

FIGURE 7

Figure 7 is a dry-sprinkler system with fire alarm monitoring initiating devices which monitor conditions on the sprinkler system.

Supervisory Initiating Devices

Supervisory initiating devices are input devices, which, when actuated, activate a supervisory condition at the fire alarm control unit. Examples of Initiating devices that produce a supervisory signal when actuated include sprinkler control valve monitoring switches, high and low air pressure switches on dry systems, and high and low water level switches for sprinkler water storage tanks.

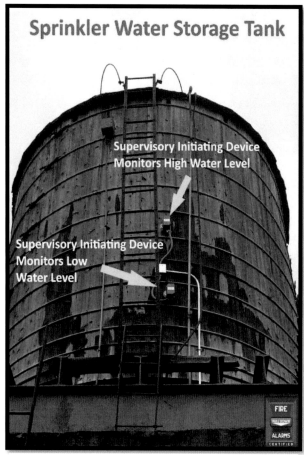

FIGURE 8   FIGURE 9

Figure 8 shows a supervisory initiating device used to monitor low water levels in a sprinkler storage tank. When the water level in the storage tank reaches a critically low level, the device is actuated and activates a supervisory signal at the fire alarm control unit alerting building personnel.

Sprinkler control valves must also be monitored by the fire alarm system. If the valve is closed, the fire alarm system must indicate a supervisory condition at the control unit. This is accomplished using an initiating device. The switching mechanism is actuated when the control valve is turned in order to close or isolate a sprinkler branch. Figure 9 shows a sprinkler control valve tamper switch supervisory initiating device.

The fire alarm system is also required to monitor high and low air conditions of a sprinkler dry system. Dry systems are used to provide fire protection in areas that are exposed to freezing temperatures such as an un-heated parking garage space. Instead of the sprinkler piping having water, the sprinkler piping is filled with pressurized air using a compressor. This pressurized air must be monitored by the fire alarm system. High and low air sensing pressure switches are used as supervisory initiating devices. When the air pressure reaches a high level or low level, the device is actuated and a supervisory condition is annunciated at the fire alarm control unit. Figure 10 and 11 below shows a high-low pressure supervisory initiating device used to monitor a dry system in a supermarket.

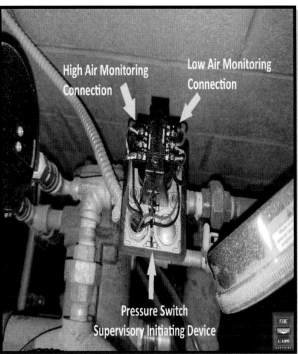

FIGURE 10

FIGURE 11

Figure 10 shows the internal connections to the pressure monitoring switch. A set of wires (black, red) are connected to the contacts that actuate in the event of high-air pressure while another set of wires are connected to the contacts that actuate when a low air pressure condition is encountered.

Supervisory initiating devices are normally open switches that close when they actuate. The closing of the switch activates the supervisory condition at the fire alarm control unit. Figure 12 shows an equivalent circuit diagram of a supervisory initiating device in the "normal" position and in the activated position. Many field technicians like to think of this closing of the switch as a shorted condition on the wiring. Though not accurate, some find this explanation easier to understand.

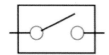
Supervisory initiating device switch "normal"

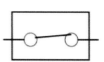
Supervisory initiating device switch "actuated"

FIGURE 12

The closing of the device switch is accomplished by the condition it is monitoring. For example, if the initiating device switch is monitoring a low water level on a sprinkler water storage tank, the float within the water tank will trigger the switch to close. This in turn, causes a supervisory condition at the fire alarm control unit.

Alarm Initiating Devices

Alarm initiating devices are similar to supervisory initiating devices as they are input devices. However, unlike supervisory initiating devices, alarm initiating devices, when activated, cause an alarm condition at the fire alarm control unit.

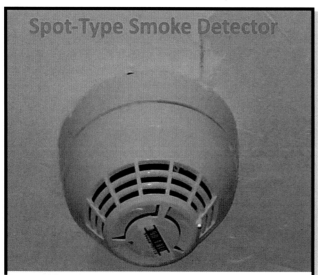
FIGURE 13

Smoke Detectors

A smoke detector is an initiating device that uses various methods of detecting smoke. There are various types of smoke detectors. One such method is using spot-type smoke detectors. Spot-type smoke detectors are installed in a general area or room. Figure 13 is an example of a spot-type smoke detector. Other methods of detecting smoke are projected-beam, air-sampling and video imaging. Each of these types are described in this chapter.

Ionization Smoke Detector

Ionization type smoke detectors contain a small amount of radioactive material. This radioactive material passes between two electrically charged plates, which in turn creates an ionization chamber. Current will flow between the plates when the air is ionized. When a fire occurs, smoke will enter the chamber, disturbing the ionization process which in turn reduces the current flow. This reduction in current is what actuates the detector. Ionization type smoke detectors are more responsive to fast, raging fire.

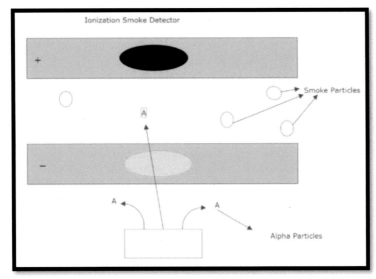

FIGURE 14

Photoelectric Smoke Detector

Photoelectric smoke detectors work by using a photoelectric sensor and a light source. The device is actuated when smoke enters the chamber and interferes with the light beam. The

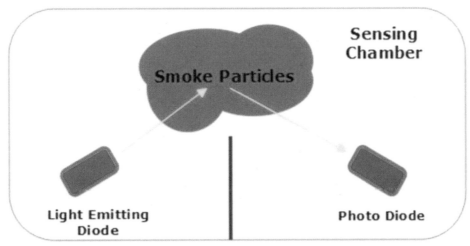

FIGURE 15

smoke particles scatter the light which is aimed at the sensor. These types of smoke detectors typically respond better to smoldering fires—essentially those that begin with a long period of smoldering.

Heat Detector

A heat detector is an initiating fire alarm device designed to activate when a fire increases the temperature of a heat sensitive element within the housing of the heat detector. There are two main types of heat detectors: rate of rise and fixed temperature. Unlike smoke detectors, heat detectors are used to protect property not people. Heat detectors are triggered when temperature rises.

FIGURE 16

Fixed temperature heat detectors are the most common type of heat detectors. Fixed temperature heat detectors activate when a specific temperature is reached or detected by the device. This closes a set of contacts in the sensor and transmits an alarm condition to the fire alarm control unit. Many times the fixed temperature sensing element is non-restorable and, when activated, the heat detector must be replaced. Figure 16 is a fixed temperature heat detector that is explosion proof installed in a gas filling station.

Rate-of-rise heat detectors activates when temperature increases or rises at a certain rate per minute. This closes the contacts in the sensor to transmit the alarm condition to the fire alarm control unit. When the rate-of-rise element alone has been activated, the sensor is self-restoring.

Heat detectors can be spot-type or linear type. Spot type heat detectors basically are installed as one unit and monitor "one spot". However, a linear heat detector looks like a cable that is fitted with an insulated jacket with a specific melting temperature. When the set temperature is reached, the insulation jacket keeping the conductors from coming in contact melts, thus the conductors short or make contact, closing the circuit and actuating an alarm.

Spot-type heat detectors use a colored ring to identify their temperature rating. NFPA 72®
table 17.6.2.1 list the temperature rating of spot-type heat detectors based on the color coding.
Figure 18 is a spot-type heat detector with a color code blue ring. Using NFPA 72® table
17.6.2.1 we can identify the temperature range of the detector as 250-324 degrees Fahrenheit.

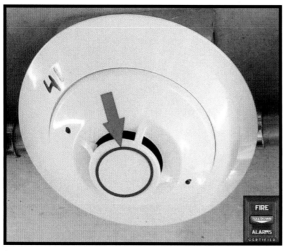

Table 17.6.2.1 Temperature Classification and Color Code for Heat-Sensing Fire Detectors

Temperature Classification	Temperature Rating Range		Maximum Ceiling Temperature		Color Code
	°F	°C	°F	°C	
Low*	100–134	39–57	80	28	Uncolored
Ordinary	135–174	58–79	115	47	Uncolored
Intermediate	175–249	80–121	155	69	White
High	250–324	122–162	230	111	Blue
Extra high	325–399	163–204	305	152	Red
Very extra high	400–499	205–259	380	194	Green
Ultra high	500–575	260–302	480	249	Orange

FIGURE 18   FIGURE 17

Reproduced with permission of NFPA from NFPA 72®, National Fire Alarm and Signaling Code®, 2016 edition. Copyright© 2015, National Fire Protection Association. For a full copy of NFPA 72®, please go to www.nfpa.org.

Air Sampling Smoke Detector

An air sampling smoke detector consists of a piping or tubing distribution network that runs
from the detector to the area or areas being protected. Air is moved through the sampling
ports on the tubing by an aspiration fan in the detector housing where the air is analyzed for fire. Air sampling smoke detectors are capable of detecting a fire at its earliest stage.

NFPA 72® requires that air-sampling

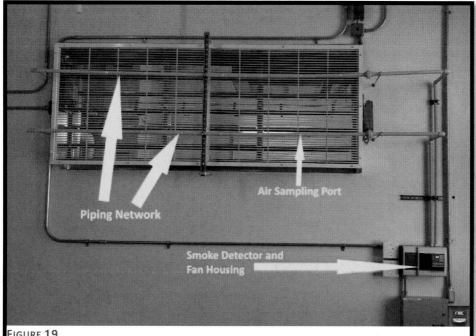

FIGURE 19

network piping and fittings be airtight and permanently fixed. At certain intervals in the network piping, NFPA 72® requires that it be identified as "SMOKE DETECTOR SAMPLING TUBE – DO NOT DISTURB"; the purpose of this is to avoid other trades from tampering with the piping. For example, a painter may not know that the network pipes are part of a smoke detection system, and simply paint over the pipes, covering the sampling ports.

Projected Bean-Type Smoke Detectors

Projected beam-type smoke detectors are used to provide "open area" smoke detection in conditions where it is usually impractical to use spot-type smoke detectors or air sampling smoke detection. Some common applications include warehouses, atriums, convention centers, shopping malls, and sports arenas.

A light is projected from the transmitter to a receiver. This light is measured, and a "normal" condition is established. When smoke enters the protected area, the smoke particles interfere with the light, obscuring the beam, causing the receiver to detect less than the "normally" established amount of light. This then causes an off-normal condition and actuates the device. Many applications use both the transmitter and receiver in one housing, and the beam is reflected at the other end. Most projected beam smoke detectors are activated when the light is partially obscured and not when fully obscured. This is to minimize false alarms caused by objects fully blocking the beam.

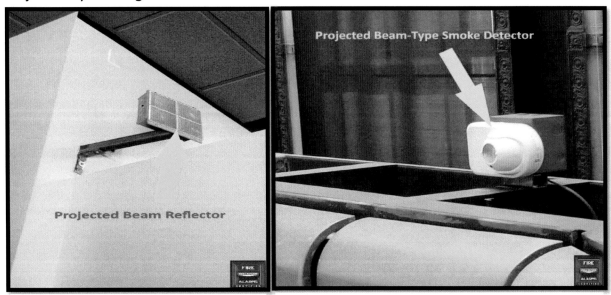

FIGURE 20   FIGURE 21

FIGURE 22

One major drawback to the use of projected beam smoke detectors is that they are susceptible to false alarms caused by objects blocking, or partially blocking the light. A shopping center used projected beam smoke detectors in an atrium space. Balloons released from shoppers would frequently partially block the transmitted light beam, causing the detector to activate.

NFPA 72® requires that the receiver and mirrors be mounted on stable surfaces to prevent misalignment which would cause false alarms.

Air-Duct Smoke Detectors

Air-duct smoke detectors are used to sample the air within a duct of HVAC systems (usually) and take appropriate action, such as shut-down said air handling unit. Air-duct smoke detectors are photoelectric spot-type smoke detectors within a housing listed specifically as duct smoke detectors. Air-duct smoke detectors detect the presence of smoke moving within the HVAC system such as smoke being transferred from another area of the building via the duct work. These detectors require the use of sampling tubes that penetrate the duct work. These sampling tubes contain ports that transfer the air to the smoke detector. Installers must ensure that the ports on the sampling tubes are facing the direction of air-flow in order to ensure the device is effective.

FIGURE 24

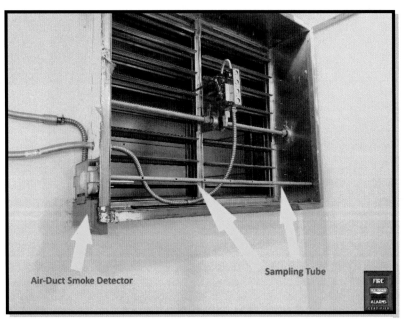

FIGURE 25

When the duct work exceeds 36 inches in width, the sampling tube must penetrate the duct work. This allows the device to properly sample a greater amount of the air travelling within the duct. NFPA 72® requires that any penetrations of a return air duct in the vicinity of the smoke detector installed on the air duct be scaled or sealed using an approved method.

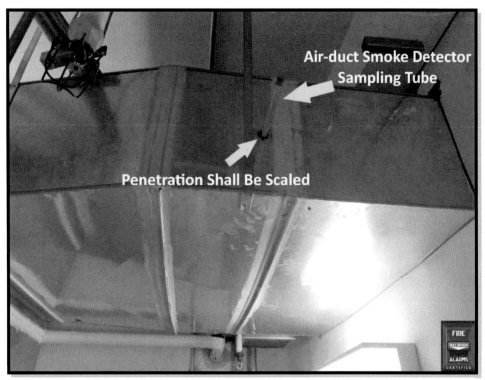

FIGURE 26

Because these detectors are usually mounted high and require the cover be removed in order to test the device using artificial smoke, test switches are sometimes installed to allow technicians to test or actuate the device by using a key.

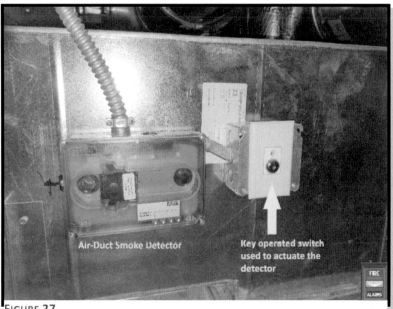

FIGURE 27

FIGURE 28

On various installations, air-duct smoke detectors are installed above the drop ceiling, not visible unless the ceiling tiles are removed. When such detectors are installed where the indicator light on the device is not visible, NFPA 72® requires that a remote lamp be provided and installed where visible to responding personnel. The remote lamp must be clearly labeled as to its function and the air-handling unit associated with such detector. Figure 28 is an example of a remote lamp installed on a ceiling for a concealed duct smoke detector. Upon activation of the smoke detector, the remote lamp LED will turn on, allowing responding personnel to identify the location of the device actuated.

Video Image Smoke/Flame Detection

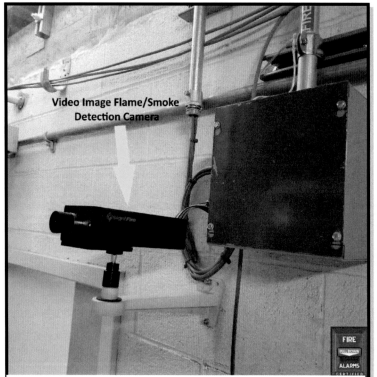

FIGURE 29

In general, a video image smoke/flame detection system consists of video cameras and computer systems that analyze the video to determine if smoke or flame is present. The detection algorithms use different techniques to identify the flame and smoke characteristics, an output alarm signal is sent to the fire alarm control unit.

The National Fire Alarm Code®, NFPA 72®, recognizes the use of video flame and smoke detection systems. Per this code, the installation of these systems requires a performance-based design. There are several advantages to these types of systems over spot-type smoke detection. One advantage video image smoke/flame detection systems offer is the ability to protect a larger area, while still achieving fast detection. Another advantage is the ability to view a live video feed of the condition by responding personnel. This allows the personnel to easily view the extent and location of the fire.

Sprinkler Water Flow Alarm-Initiating Device

Sprinkler waterflow monitoring is accomplished using a waterflow device. Waterflow initiating devices detect continuous flow of water through the fire sprinkler system piping due to an activated sprinkler head. The waterflow detector is made up of a plastic vane or paddle that is installed through an opening on the fire sprinkler pipe (see diagram below), either vertically or horizontally. When water begins to flow through such sprinkler piping, the vane or paddle triggers a switch transmitting an alarm signal to the fire alarm control unit.

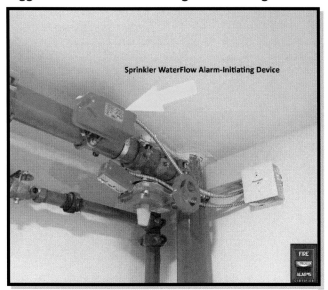

FIGURE 31

Valve

FIGURE 30

FIGURE 32

The waterflow device has a feature that allows a delay to be set by the installer. This delay is meant to allow the device to transmit the alarm signal within a few seconds after the flow of water to minimize false alarms caused by movement of the water within the sprinkler piping. Movement of water within the sprinkler (unassociated with an open sprinkler head do to a fire) can be caused by waste, surges or a difference in water pressure. NFPA 72® specifies that the alarm condition shall be initiated within 90 seconds of the flow of water, however, enough time must be given due to movement of water due to conditions not associated with an open sprinkler head to not initiate an alarm condition. Usually, installers will set the delay between 30 seconds and 45 seconds of the flow of water. This is done by adjusting a dial on the device itself (figure 32).

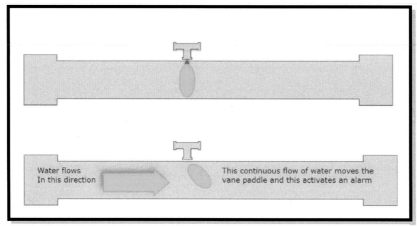

Figure 33 shows the waterflow device's paddle within the sprinkler piping. Upon the flow of water, the paddle is shifted which activates a switch within the housing. After a set amount of time the water flow device will actuate or close a set of contacts which will indicate an alarm condition at the fire alarm control unit.

Manually Actuated Alarm-Initiating Device

Manual fire alarm activation is typically accomplished through the use of a manual pull station. Different from other fire alarm initiating devices (smoke, heat detectors, and sprinkler waterflow) which are activated via automatic means, manual pull station activation requires human intervention.

To activate the manual pull station the user simply pulls the handle down, which completes a circuit and locks the handle in the activated position. An alarm signal is transmitted to the fire alarm control unit. Most manual pull stations require the device be reset to its normal position before the fire alarm control unit can be reset.

NFPA 72® requires that manual fire alarm pull stations be installed so that they are unobstructed and accessible. Many times manual pull stations are covered by book cases or other furniture after the installation. NFPA 72® requires that manual fire alarm pull stations be red in color. Listed protective covers are allowed to be used on manual pull stations, but they must be listed for the device. Some protective covers have small batteries that connect to a mini-horn. When the protective cover is lifted (to give access to the manual pull station), a local buzzer sounds. This is meant to deter false alarms from occupants intentionally activating the manual pull station without actually witnessing a fire condition.

Manual pull stations are permitted (by NFPA 72®) to be of a single action type or double action type. Single action manual pull stations require only one action to activate (pulling of the handle), while double action require an action prior to pulling the handle; such as lifting a cover.

FIGURE 34

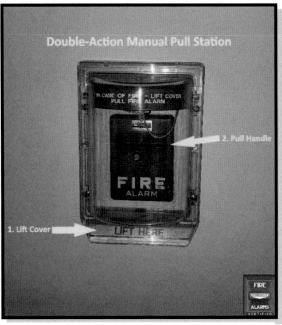

FIGURE 35

FIGURE 36

NFPA 72® specifies the mounting height requirements and location of manual fire alarm pull stations. NFPA 72® requires manual fire alarm pull stations be installed so that the operable part of the device (the handle) be no less than 42 inches and not more than 48 inches from the floor. Usually, local laws and building codes require different mounting heights due to persons with disabilities. In addition, NFPA 72® requires that when manual fire alarm pull stations are installed, they shall be located within 60 inches from the exit doorway on each floor.

Addressable vs. Conventional Initiating Devices

Conventional initiating devices connect to the initiating device circuit. These devices are "dumb" devices, they require no programming and simply work by opening or closing a set of contacts, which changes the current in the circuit letting the control unit know there was a change, and causing the outputs (example: horns and strobes) to activate. Conventional initiating devices can only report by zones and not by individual device.

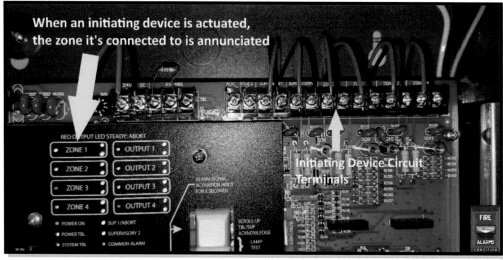

FIGURE 37

Addressable initiating devices connect to the signaling line circuit (SLC). These devices must be programmed into the control units and given an address. Using this "address", the system can identify the exact device that initiated the signal and thus identifying its location in the premises. For example, if there are 5 addressable smoke detectors on a signaling line circuit, if the smoke detector in the electrical room actuates, the fire alarm control unit (FACU) will annunciate the exact location of the alarm or the actuated initiating device.

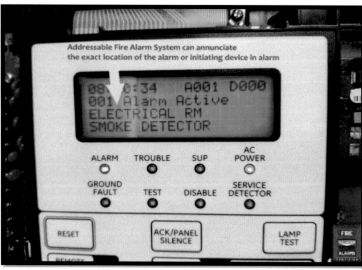

FIGURE 38

Addressable initiating devices can be programmed using special equipment supplied by the manufacturer. Figure 39 shows a fire alarm device programming unit. The fire alarm device programming unit assigns an address to a smoke/heat/CO detector. The installer places the device onto the unit, then proceeds to program the device. After the device has been programmed, the device can be permanently installed in the field.

Conventional devices can be "connected" to an addressable fire alarm system using input monitoring modules. These monitoring modules take an input from an input device, such as a pressure switch, and "convert" this into data that is then transmitted to the fire alarm control unit.

FIGURE 39

Notification Appliances

Notification appliances are defined by NFPA 72® as "a fire alarm system component such as a bell, horn, speaker, light, or text display that provides audible, tactile, or visible outputs, or any

combination thereof."

Notification appliances are output devices that are used to alert the occupants in a building or premises that there is a fire condition or off-

FIGURE 40

normal condition on the system. Notification appliances include the following: bells, strobes, horn strobes, speakers, multi tone bells, and chimes.

Bells are notification appliances that connect to the notification appliance circuit. Bells generally are supplied in sizes ranging from 4 inches to 12 inches. Normally, water flow bells are the biggest, followed by the smoke bell, and then the trouble bell is the smallest. Bells are normally set up to sound in a continuous fashion, either vibrating or stroke kind.

FIGURE 41

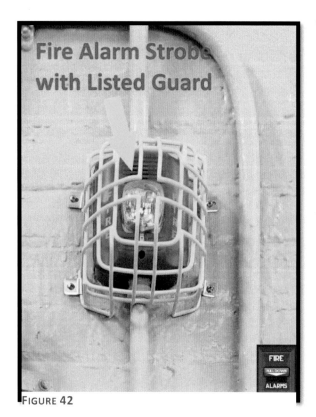

FIGURE 42

Visible alarm notification, also known as strobes, are output devices that connect to the notification appliance circuit; they begin flashing when activated by the fire alarm control unit. Strobes are normally wall mounted, but there are ceiling type strobes. According to NFPA 72®, wall mounted visible appliances should be installed between 96 inches and 80 inches from the floor. The candela is the standard unit used to measure light intensity. The higher the candela rating of a strobe, the more intense the light. NFPA 72® requires that, at a minimum, visible notification appliances be rated at 15 candelas or cd.

Figure 42 shows a fire alarm visible notification appliance, strobe, mounted with a listed guard in a high school gymnasium. The purpose of the guard is to protect the appliance from flying debris. NFPA 72® chapter 18 specifies that appliances subject to mechanical damage be suitably protected. This protection, such as the guard, shall be listed for use with the appliance. NFPA 72® defines the light, color and pulse characteristics of the visible notification appliance. NFPA 72® chapter 18 requires that strobes' flash rate to not exceed 2 flashes per second, nor be less than 1 flash per second. Lights used for fire alarm signaling only or those used to evacuate occupants shall be clear or nominal white and shall not exceed 1000 cd (effective intensity).

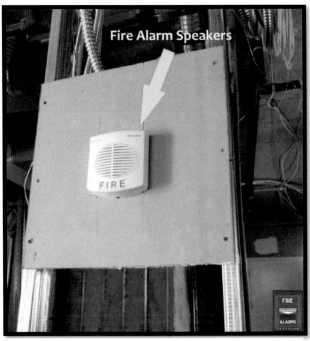

FIGURE 43

Speakers are normally used with voice / alarm communication systems. With this system, announcements can be made to the occupants, for example, to alert them that they need to evacuate due to fire or any other emergency situation. Figure 43 shows a speaker installed in an apartment of a high-rise residential apartment building. NFPA 72® chapter 18 specifies that wall mounted audible notification appliances shall have their tops above the finished floors at heights of not less than 90 in. and below the finished ceilings at distances of not less than 6 in.

FIGURE 44

These audible devices usually have dip switches that allow the installer to increase the wattage of the device to achieve a higher audible signal, if desired or required, to meet NFPA® requirements.

Combination visible/audible notification appliances (horn/strobe) are output devices that connect to the notification appliance circuit. A horn/strobe has two functions; produce a visible alarm signal and an audible alarm signal. According to NFPA 72®, combination audible/visible appliances, such as a horn/strobe, will be mounted according to the requirements of visible appliances.

Notification appliances can be installed on the ceiling of a room, however, NFPA 72® sets maximum height requirements for such installations. Figure 44 shows a horn/strobe installed in a supermarket. In order to provide alarm notification, ceiling mounted devices were required to be used. When ceiling heights exceed 30 feet, NFPA 72® requires ceiling mounted visible devices be suspended at or below 30 feet.

NFPA 72® requires that the alarm audible signal pattern used to notify building occupants of the need to evacuate the building or relocate (from one area to another) to be the standard alarm evacuation signal consisting of a three-pulse temporal pattern. This evacuation audible signal consist of an "ON" sound lasting for 0.5 seconds, no sound for 0.5 seconds, an "ON" sound lasting 0.5 seconds, no sound for 0.5 seconds, an "ON" sound for 0.5 seconds, then no sound lasting 1.5 seconds until the pattern is repeated again. This pattern is recognized as the temporal-3 pattern. This temporal-3 signal shall be repeated for at least 180 seconds. Generally, the temporal-3 pattern is repeated until user intervention causes the signal to be silenced. Silencing the signal is accomplished by pressing a button at the fire alarm control unit.

NFPA 72® requires that the temporal-3 evacuation signal be synchronized within a notification zone. If there are 2 or more audible notification appliances located within the same room or area, the temporal-3 evacuation signal shall be synchronized. The evacuation signal is meant to notify not confuse building occupants. Not syncing the audible signal within the same notification zone will cause disorientation to the occupants, defeating the purpose of the evacuation signal. Synchronization of the audible signal within a notification zone is required to preserve the temporal-3 pattern.

QUESTIONS

1. Which of the following components make up a fire alarm system?
   a. Relays
   b. Notification appliances
   c. Initiating devices
   d. All of the above

2. The fire alarm control unit (FACU) is usually powered by _____.
   a. 120 VAC
   b. 24 VDC
   c. 12 VDC
   d. None of the above

3. Is the following statement true or false: Initiating devices, such as smoke detectors, water flows, or pull stations are output devices
   a. True
   b. False

4. Which of the following is not an output device?
   a. Strobe
   b. Fan Shutdown relay
   c. Pressure switch
   d. Door release relay
   e. None of the above

5. Smoke detectors, supervisory switches and pull stations are connected to which circuit?
   a. IDC
   b. NAC
   c. Both A & B
   d. None of the above

6. Which of the following isn't a supervisory initiating device?
   a. Tamper valve or switch
   b. Water flow device
   c. High / Low pressure switch
   d. None of the above

7. Is the following statement true or false? If the fire alarm control unit (FACU) indicates that a sprinkler control valve is off-normal, this means that the valve is closed.
   a. True
   b. False

8. In a sprinkler storage tank, if the water level reaches a low point, the FACP will indicate:
   a. Alarm signal
   b. Trouble signal
   c. No signal
   d. Supervisory signal

9. Is the following statement true or false? High / low pressure switches are used to monitor sprinkler dry system.
   a. True
   b. False

10. If a high / low pressure switch activates, the FACU will indicate a(an) _____.
    a. Supervisory signal
    b. Trouble signal
    c. Alarm signal
    d. All of the above

11. What type of smoke detector activates when smoke enters the chamber and interferes with the light beam.
    a. Ionization smoke detector
    b. Air sampling smoke detector
    c. Projected beam type smoke detector
    d. Photoelectric smoke Detector

12. Is the following statement true or false: Ionization smoke detectors are more responsive to fast, raging fire?
    a. False
    b. True

13. Which type of fire alarm system uses data to communicate with the initiating devices?
    a. Addressable
    b. Conventional
    c. None of the above

14. Which type of smoke detector detects the presence of smoke within the HVAC system?
    a. Projected beam type smoke detector
    b. Video image smoke detector
    c. Air duct smoke detector
    d. None of the above

15. If a water flow device activates this will transmit what type of signal?
    a. Alarm
    b. Supervisory
    c. Trouble
    d. None of the above

16. According to NFPA 72®, a water flow switch shall activate within _____ of the flow of water.
    a. 10 seconds
    b. 90 seconds
    c. 180 seconds
    d. 270 seconds
    e. None of the above

17. Is the following statement true or false? The end of line resistor can be installed on any device on an initiating device circuit.
    a. True
    b. False

18. Is the following statement true or false? According to NFPA 72®, manual pull stations can either be single action or double action type.
    a. False
    b. True

19. Manual pull stations are input devices or output devices?
    a. Input devices
    b. Output devices
    c. Both A and B
    d. None of the above

20. According to NFPA 72®, manual fire alarm pull stations shall be installed so that the operable part of the device (the handle) shall be no less than ___ inches and not more than ___ inches from the floor.
    a. 42 and 42
    b. 48 and 42
    c. 42 and 48
    d. 36 and 42

Chapter 3

OBJECTIVES:

➢ Understand the wiring diagram of an initiating device circuit.

➢ Understand how the purpose of the end-of-line resistor.

➢ Understand the wiring diagram of the notification appliance circuit.

➢ Understand the signaling line circuit.

➢ Discuss monitoring modules and control modules.

Fire Alarm Circuit Wiring Diagrams

This chapter will focus on wiring diagrams to explain how a zoned/conventional fire alarm system works, as well as how the notification appliance outputs are activated when an alarm condition is received.

Initiating Device Circuit

The initiating device circuit is used to connect initiating devices in the field to the fire alarm control unit. The fire alarm control unit (conventional – zoned system) will contain contacts labeled zones or IDCs where the initiating device circuit is connected. Initiating devices are simply switches that close to indicate an actuated condition. Under "normal" operating conditions the initiating devices are open. For example, when a (conventional) smoke detector detects smoke, a set of contacts are closed and the circuit resistance is changed. This change in resistance changes the amount of current flow in the circuit which indicates that an alarm condition has occurred. The fire alarm control unit will then proceed with the programmed response (activate the horns and strobes, transmit a signal to the central monitoring station).

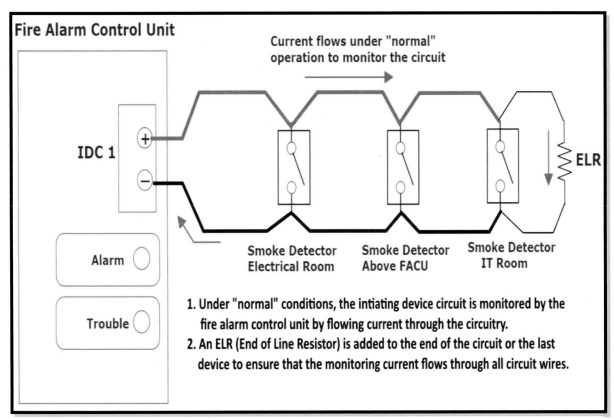

FIGURE 45

Figure 45 shows an initiating device circuit under "normal" operating conditions.

When a smoke detector (conventional) is actuated, contacts are closed within the device. This changes the current flow in the circuitry, indicating an alarm condition. Figure 46 shows the smoke detector in the electrical room actuated via closing of the normally open contacts.

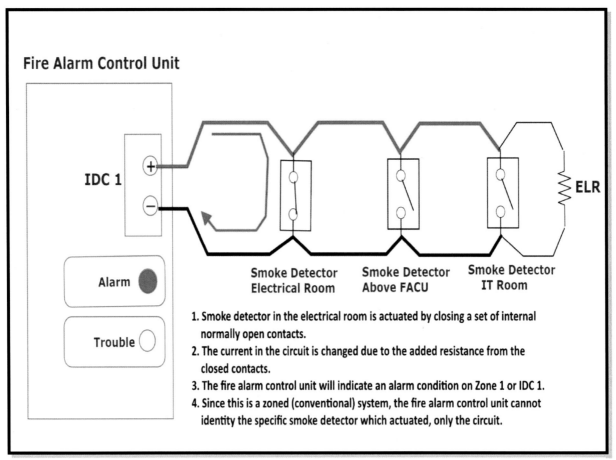

Fire Alarm Control Unit

IDC 1

ELR

Alarm

Trouble

Smoke Detector
Electrical Room

Smoke Detector
Above FACU

Smoke Detector
IT Room

1. Smoke detector in the electrical room is actuated by closing a set of internal normally open contacts.
2. The current in the circuit is changed due to the added resistance from the closed contacts.
3. The fire alarm control unit will indicate an alarm condition on Zone 1 or IDC 1.
4. Since this is a zoned (conventional) system, the fire alarm control unit cannot identity the specific smoke detector which actuated, only the circuit.

FIGURE 46

Monitoring of the circuit is accomplished by applying current. If the circuit is completed, then current will flow through the wiring. If the fire alarm control unit detects no current in the circuit, this indicates an open circuit, and a trouble will be annunciated at the control unit. Figure 47 shows an open circuit in the wiring between the smoke detector above the fire alarm control unit, and the smoke detector in the IT room.

It is important to understand why the end of line resistor (ELR) must be installed at the end of the circuit. It is evident that if we relocated the ELR to either the smoke detector in the electrical room or the smoke detector above the FACU, an open at the current location would not be annunciated as a trouble condition at the fire alarm control unit because current would still flow through the circuit. Placing the end of line resistor anywhere other than the end of the circuit will result in a circuit which is not truly monitored for open.

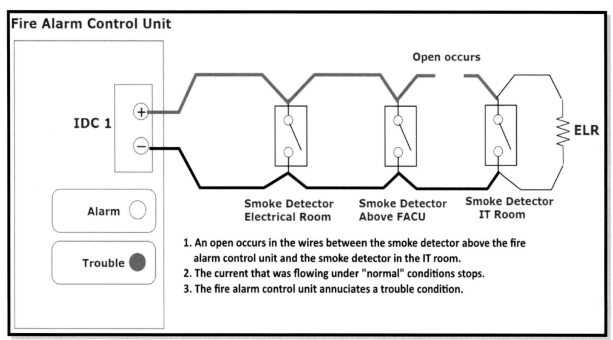

FIGURE 47

Notification Appliance Circuit

The notification appliance circuit relies on a diode on each notification appliance. A diode simply allows current to flow in one direction, depending on whether the diode is forward biased or reversed biased.

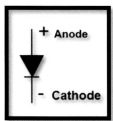

FIGURE 48

A diode is an electrical component that allows current to flow in only one direction. When the diode is forward biased, current can flow through the diode. When the diode is reverse-biased, no current flows through the diode. In other words, when a positive polarity is applied to the anode of the diode, current will flow, if a positive is applied to the cathode of the diode, current will not flow.

When placed in a simple battery-lamp circuit, the diode will either allow or prevent current through the lamp, depending on the polarity of the applied voltage.

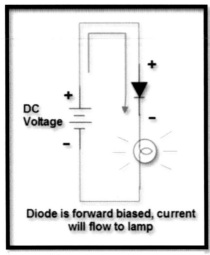

Diode is forward biased, current will flow to lamp

FIGURE 49

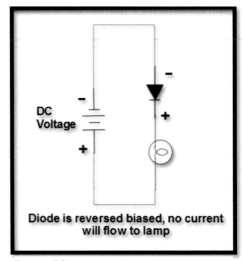

Diode is reversed biased, no current will flow to lamp

FIGURE 50

The figures 49 and 50 shows what happens to the current flow in the circuit when the diode is forward-biased and reverse-biased by changing the polarity of the voltage source. The same principle is applied to the notification appliance circuit to activate the notification appliances. A notification appliance can be represented on a wiring diagram by a diode in series with the circuitry required to operate the appliance.

Making sure that polarities are connected properly is extremely important when wiring notification appliance circuits. The standard wiring model is to use the red color conductor as the positive and the black color conductor as the negative. The notification appliances' terminals will be marked + and – respectively. The installer must assure that red is landed on positive and black on negative.

Figure 51 shows a notification appliance circuit under normal operating conditions. No current flows through any of the horns/strobe due to the diode. Notice how there is current flowing through the circuit due to the end of line resistor. This current is used to monitor the wiring for opens; such as if one of the horns/strobes are removed.

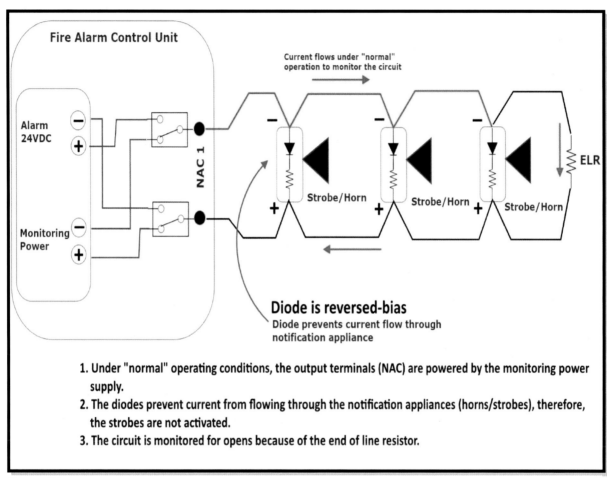

FIGURE 51

Under an alarm condition, the fire alarm control unit will switch the NAC terminals to the alarm power supply. Figure 52 shows that the polarity of these terminals are reversed, current in the circuit will flow in the opposite direction, voltage is applied to the notification appliances, the horn will sound, and the strobes will flash.

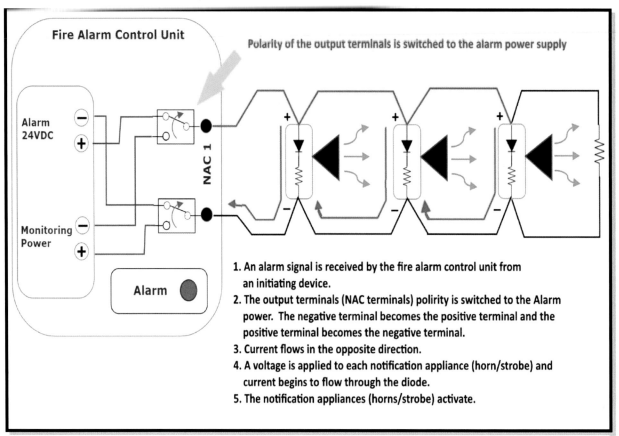

FIGURE 52

Signaling Line Circuit

Addressable fire alarm systems use signaling line circuits (SLC); usually referred to as loops. Depending on the protocol used, a signaling line circuit can monitor and control several hundred devices and even a thousand devices. The SLC "polls" or communicates with the devices on the circuit to make sure that they are "connected". Each device on the SLC has its own assigned address. The address is identified by a programmer as to the location of the device. The fire alarm control unit knows where each device is located and what type of device it is (smoke detector, heat detector, input/output module).

When a smoke detector activates, data is sent to the fire alarm control unit. The FACU knows exactly which device actuated the alarm and annunciates it on the display. This allows responding personnel to quickly identify the location of the fire. In contrast to a conventional-zoned system, which can only identify the zone that actuated the alarm; the zone can be many devices on that circuit in different rooms.

Figure 53 is of an addressable system under "normal" conditions. The fire alarm control unit is constantly polling the devices on the circuit to monitor their condition. It shall be noted that no end of line resistor is used since the monitoring isn't accomplished using standard current flow, but rather using data interchange between the FACU and the devices acknowledging that they are present in the circuit.

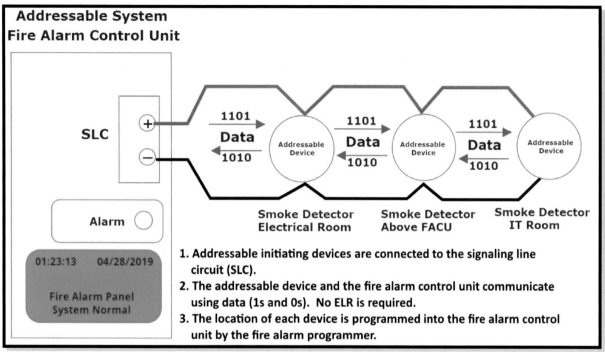

Figure 54 shows what happens when one of the devices on the circuit goes into an alarm condition. The device transmits an alarm signal to the FACU. The fire alarm control unit then annunciates the alarm and the exact location of the device actuated on its display.

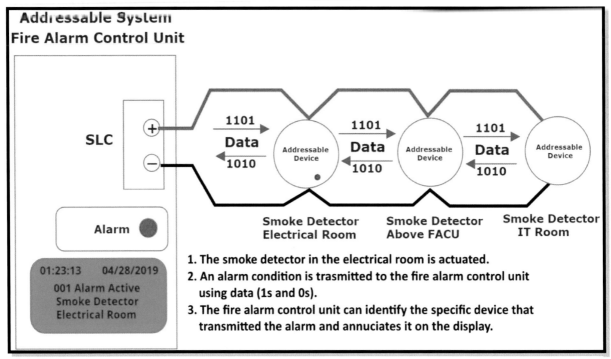

FIGURE 54

The beauty of this type of system is that many devices can just be added to the loop. There is no need to add devices after the last device since monitoring of the circuit is not done through "brute" current flow, but rather through "intelligent" communication between the initiating devices and the fire alarm control unit.

Conventional devices can also be added to an addressable system's SLC loop using monitoring modules. For example, a water flow switch can be connected to the SLC loop but must be first interfaced using a monitoring module. In its simplest form, a monitoring module monitors an open or closed position on one side, and outputs data on the other. Since a water flow device doesn't output data, it needs to be connected to a device that can output data. Figure 55 is of a water flow device connected to a monitoring module which is connected to the SLC loop. When the water flow activates by closing its normally open contact, the current flow changes. This change is detected by the monitoring module, which in turn, transmits a data signal through the SLC loop to the addressable fire alarm control unit. The monitoring module is assigned an address and the address is given a description. In this situation, the description given to the monitoring module is that of the device it is monitoring: water-flow switch. When the water flow activates, the fire alarm control unit will annunciate "water flow device" on its display.

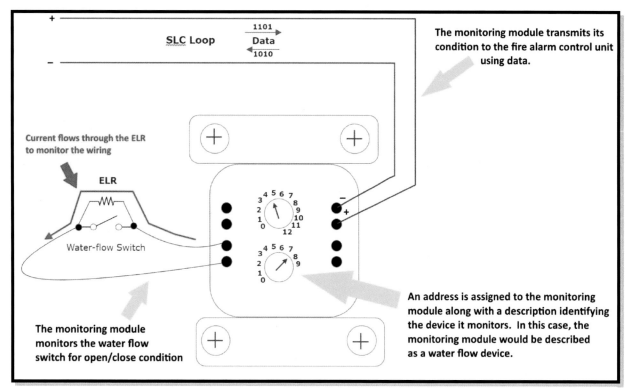

FIGURE 55

In order to control non-fire alarm equipment, such as shutting down a fan or closing the louvers on a fire smoke damper, an input-output control module can be used. Typically, to shut-down a fan, a circuit within the fan unit must be interrupted, or switched. The fire alarm control unit can "interface" with the controls of the HVAC system using what are typically known as control modules. A control module receives a signal from the fire alarm control unit to either open or close the circuit it wishes to control. Since the control module receives a signal from the fire alarm control unit, it is considered an output device. The description assigned to the particular control module is the function it is trying to accomplish. If a control module is used to operate or open a fire smoke damper, the module's description will then be "fire smoke damper".

Figure 57 shows a control module that can be used to control functions (on/off, open/close) on equipment. Figure 56 is an installation of fire smoke dampers at the top of the stair case of a residential apartment building. The fire smoke dampers installed are to open upon activation of a smoke detector at the top of the stairs. This is accomplished by using control modules and high-voltage relays to interface the signaling line circuit with the fire smoke dampers.

FIGURE 57

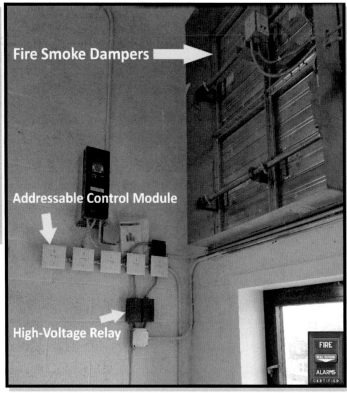

FIGURE 56

Control modules can be used to interface with the following building functions or systems:

- Transmit an output signal to the elevator controller to recall the elevators
- Shut-down escalators
- Release electrically held doors
- Activate exhaust fans to provide post fire smoke purge function
- Shut-down supply fans
- Activate stair pressurization fans
- Activate or close fire shutter doors
- Activate or deactivate power to a solenoid
- Shut-down fuel supply pump

Similar to monitoring modules, control modules are assigned an address so that the fire alarm control unit can "activate" it, and the function intended can be achieved.

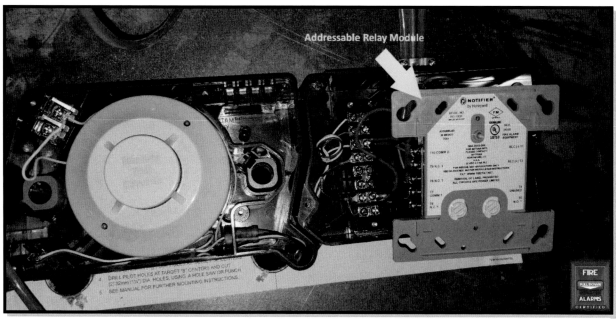

FIGURE 58

Figure 58 is of an addressable relay module, or control module, used to shut-down an air handling unit on the roof of a medical office. The module is programmed or given an address. Upon activation of an alarm condition, the fire alarm control unit sends a data signal to the addressable module which disconnects or opens the HVAC control loop going to the air handling unit.

Figure 59 is of a simple circuit demonstrating how an addressable relay module is used to shut off a controlled equipment external to the fire alarm system. Under normal conditions, the light is energized by the external power source. This external power source is looped through the common and normally closed (NC) contacts on the addressable relay module. When the fire alarm control unit receives an alarm condition from a field device, such as a smoke detector, the programming or correlation will send a signal to the addressable relay module to activate. Activation basically means to open the connection or contacts so that the current flowing through to the load stops, thus shutting down the controlled equipment. This controlled equipment can be any equipment we wish the fire alarm system to control, such as a supply fan.

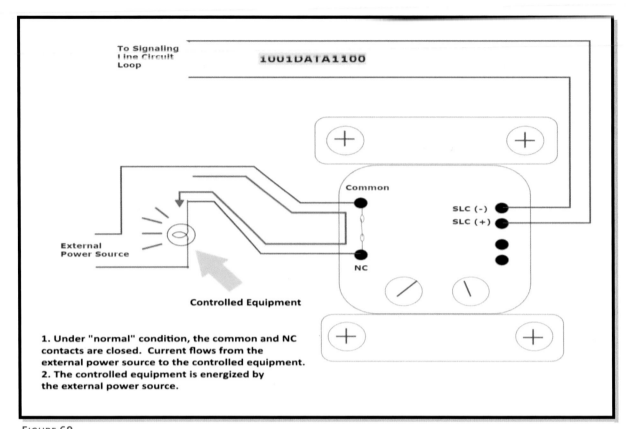

To Signaling Line Circuit Loop

1001DATA1100

Common

SLC (-)
SLC (+)

External Power Source

NC

Controlled Equipment

1. Under "normal" condition, the common and NC contacts are closed. Current flows from the external power source to the controlled equipment.
2. The controlled equipment is energized by the external power source.

FIGURE 60

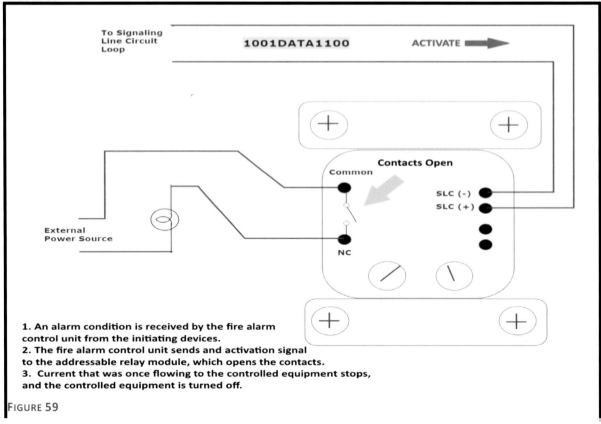

To Signaling Line Circuit Loop

1001DATA1100

ACTIVATE ➡

Contacts Open

Common

SLC (-)
SLC (+)

External Power Source

NC

1. An alarm condition is received by the fire alarm control unit from the initiating devices.
2. The fire alarm control unit sends and activation signal to the addressable relay module, which opens the contacts.
3. Current that was once flowing to the controlled equipment stops, and the controlled equipment is turned off.

FIGURE 59

QUESTIONS

Use the following wiring diagram to answer questions 1 – 5.

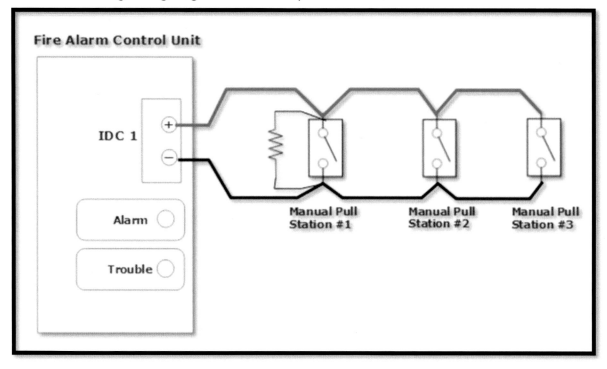

1. True or False. An open circuit between manual pull station #1 and #2 will result in a trouble condition at the fire alarm control unit.
   a. True
   b. False

2. True of False. An open circuit between manual pull station #2 and #3 will result in a trouble condition at the fire alarm control unit.
   a. True.
   b. False.

3. True or False. An open circuit between the fire alarm control unit and manual pull station #1 will result in a trouble condition at the fire alarm control unit.
   a. True
   b. False

4. If an open circuit exist between manual pull station #2 and #3, and manual pull station #2 is actuated, the fire alarm control unit will _____ .
   a. Indicate an alarm condition.
   b. Indicate a trouble condition.
   c. Indicate both a trouble condition and an alarm condition.

5. If the end of line resistor is removed from the circuit, the fire alarm control unit will _____.
   a. Indicate an alarm condition.
   b. Indicate a trouble condition.
   c. Indicate both a trouble condition and an alarm condition.

6. For class B style wiring, the end-of-line resistor should always be installed _____.
   a. At the first device.
   b. At the last device.
   c. At the fire alarm control unit terminals.

7. A diode is an electrical component which _____.
   a. Doesn't allow current flow.
   b. Blocks voltage.
   c. Only allows current to flow in one direction.
   d. Generates electrical current.

8. Signaling line circuits are used to connect _____.
   a. Horns and strobes
   b. Initiating devices
   c. DC voltage sources
   d. AC Voltage

9. True or False. The signaling line circuit uses an end of line resistor to monitor the circuit.
   a. True
   b. False

10. Monitoring modules are used to _____.
    a. Provide monitoring of conventional initiating devices.
    b. Provide power to notification appliances.
    c. Shut-down building equipment such as fans.
    d. Provide power to the fire alarm control unit.

Chapter 4

OBJECTIVES:

➤ Understand the difference between PLFA circuits and NPLFA circuits.

➤ Discuss the National Electrical Code® and how it applies to fire alarm installations.

➤ Explain height and mounting requirements permitted by the National Electrical Code®.

The National Electrical Code® (NFPA® 70 - NEC) contains requirements that set the foundation for electrical safety in residential, commercial, and industrial occupancies. The NEC® is broken up into articles, sections and chapters. Article 760 of the National Electrical Code® covers the installation of wiring and equipment of fire alarm systems including all circuits controlled and powered by the fire alarm system. Though NEC® article 760 covers most fire alarm installations, other articles and sections of the NEC® are applicable when installing fire alarm systems. For example, when providing wiring for fan shut-down, article 725 shall be consulted. In this chapter we will cover the sections of the NEC® which are more likely to be encountered by a fire alarm installer. All sections quoted will be based off the 2014 cycle of the NEC®. Keep in mind that different jurisdictions (cities, towns, states) will adopt a different cycle of the NEC®.

The National Electrical Code® dedicates section 760.2 to define certain terms used in article 760. For example, The NEC® defines an abandoned fire alarm cable as not identified for future use with a tag and not terminated at equipment at either end.

Often a job or installation includes removal of an older fire alarm system to be replaced with a newer fire alarm system. In this installation, all fire alarm cables are replaced with newer cables. The abandoned cables are those that will not be used for future use. Portions of this older, abandoned fire alarm cables must be removed as per NEC® 760.25.

The NEC® classifies fire alarm circuits as either non-power limited or power limited fire alarm circuits. Fire alarm circuits includes the conductors on the load side of the overcurrent protection device (fuse or circuit breaker) and the circuit conductors that are controlled by the fire alarm system.

Fire alarm circuits are basically the wiring that supply power (usually 120VAC) to the fire alarm control unit, as well as the wiring that connect the field devices (smoke detectors, heat detectors, horns and strobes) to the fire alarm control unit.

Figure 61 is an installation of a fire alarm control unit. The wiring or circuit on the

FIGURE 61

FIGURE 62

load side of the fused disconnect switch is defined as the non-power limited fire alarm circuit, while the wiring connected to the field devices (manual pull stations, smoke detectors, etc.) is the power-limited fire alarm circuits.

NEC® article 760.3(K) specifies that when fire alarm cables emerge from a raceway used for mechanical support or protection, a bushing shall be used to protect the cable. Figure 62 is a visual of this section in action. The bushing protects the cable from damage. Care must also be taken during the installation process; specifically, when cables are pulled through the conduit or raceway.

NEC® 760.24 mandates that fire alarm circuits be installed in a neat and workmanlike manner. This section applies to both wiring within panels and circuits ran exposed along walls. Wiring terminated within control units or terminated on fire alarm equipment

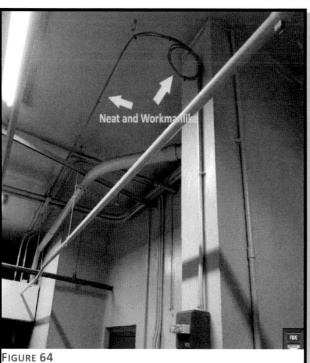

Neat and Workmanlike

FIGURE 64

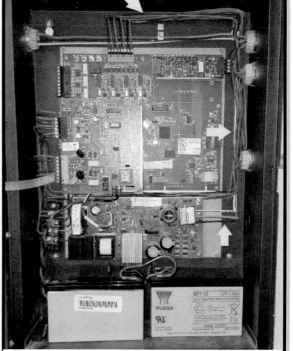

FIGURE 63

Identified for future use with tag

FIGURE 65

shall be neatly installed; no slack should be left on the runs. Cables shall be installed or mounted to walls in a manner that they will not be damaged by normal building use. A good practice is to bundle the fire alarm cables together and run them as tight as possible mounted to walls.

NEC® 760.25 covers abandoned fire alarm cables and cables used for future use. When fire alarm cables are used for future use, they shall be identified as such with a tag. This ensures that the cables aren't removed by another trade or by the building personnel.

NEC® 760.30 specifies that fire alarm circuits be identified at terminals and junction locations in a manner that helps to prevent unintentional signals on fire alarm system circuit(s) during testing and servicing of other systems. Identification can be accomplished by labeling the terminal and junction boxes with the words "Fire Alarm Circuits" or by other means as required by the local authority having jurisdiction (Figure 66). In NYC, covers of boxes, enclosures or cabinets shall be painted red and identified. This ensures that other trades, during installation, don't use boxes, enclosures or cabinets housing the fire alarm cables to install circuits that are foreign to the fire alarm system.

Often other trades use existing enclosures which are dedicated to the fire alarm system circuits to install circuits. If a fault occurs in the circuit it can affect the operation of the fire alarm system.

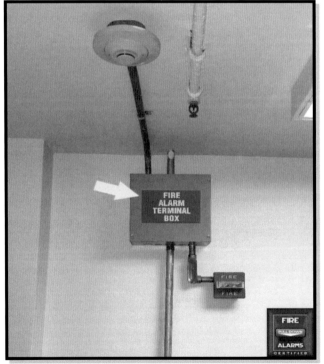

FIRE ALARM TERMINAL BOX

FIGURE 66

NEC® 760.41 covers the installation requirements for the power source that feeds the fire alarm system. The NEC® specifies that the fire alarm system shall be supplied by a dedicated branch circuit that feeds no other loads. This is done to ensure that the integrity of the circuit is maintained. A fault caused by another system shouldn't affect the power to the fire alarm system. The circuit disconnect (circuit breaker or fused disconnect switch) is permitted to be locked in the "on" position. This is meant to ensure that the fire alarm circuit isn't inadvertently disconnected. In addition, the circuit disconnect means shall have red identification and be labeled "FIRE ALARM CIRCUIT".

A placard must be placed on the fire alarm control unit indicating the location of the overcurrent protection device. Usually, a placard is placed on the FACU indicating "Disconnect means located in cellar-electrical room". In the event that the system must be powered down, the location of where to do so must be identified.

The circuit conductors connected on the load side of the overcurrent protection device shall be copper only. Conductors can either be solid or stranded and shall be protected by an

FIGURE 67

FIGURE 68

overcurrent protection device not to exceed the conductor's ampacity value.

To ensure that power to the fire alarm system is not opened by faults caused from faulty equipment or from small faults, NEC® 760.41(B) specifies that the branch circuit shall not be supplied through ground-fault circuit interrupters or arc-fault circuit interrupters.

Power-limited fire alarm circuits (PLFA circuits) are (usually) the circuits that connect from the fire alarm control unit to the field devices. Where PLFA circuits are installed exposed, cables shall be adequately supported and installed in such a way that maximum protection against physical damage is afforded by building construction. Where located within 2.1 m (7 ft) of the floor, cables shall be securely fastened in an approved manner at intervals of not more than 450 mm (18 in.).

Support of PLFA cables shall be in accordance with NEC® 760.127(B); which requires cables within 7 feet of the finished floor be supported at intervals not exceeding 18 inches. In addition, NEC® 760.143 does not allow Power-limited fire alarm circuit conductors to be strapped, taped, or attached by any means to the exterior of any conduit or other raceway as a means of support. Cables shall be installed in metal raceways or rigid nonmetallic conduit where passing through a floor or wall to a height of 2.1 m (7 ft) above the floor. Figure 70 is of an installation of a fire alarm system in a shopping center. Power limited fire alarm cables installed below 7 feet shall be installed in a metal raceway or rigid nonmetallic raceway. This is meant to protect the fire alarm cables from physical damage due to normal building operations.

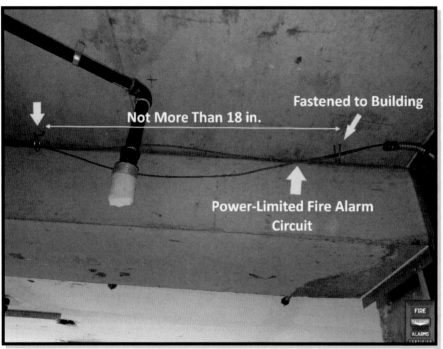

FIGURE 69

FIGURE 70

In certain areas where the fire alarm cables are installed, they shall be in a raceway regardless of the height to the floor. For example, NEC® 760.127(B)(3) specifies that power limited fire alarm cables installed in hoistways must be installed in rigid metal conduit, rigid nonmetallic conduit, intermediate metal conduit, or electrical metallic tubing. This is to offer maximum protection to the cables within hoistways. The NEC® defines a hoistway as any shaftway, hatchway, well hole, or other vertical opening or space in which an elevator or dumbwaiter is designed to operate. The cables that connect to the smoke detector at the top of the elevator hoistway or shaft must then be installed in a raceway regardless of how high it is off of the floor.

Figure 72 is of an installation of a smoke detector at the top of the elevator shaft or hoistway in a low rise residential apartment building. The power limited fire alarm circuit cables are installed in EMT to provide protection from physical damage.

Figure 71 shows power limited fire alarm cables strapped to EMT. NEC® 760.143 strictly prohibits this because the cables should be independently supported to the building structure. If in the future the building owner decided to remove the EMT conduit to which the fire alarm cable is currently supported by, the worker removing the EMT will also disturb the fire alarm cable; possibly even damaging the cable and causing any device connected to that circuit to be disconnected from the fire alarm system.

FIGURE 71

Smoke Detector at Top of Elevator Shaft

NPLFA Circuit Installed in Conduit

FIGURE 72

The NEC® describes the different types of power limited fire alarm cables and where they are permitted to be installed. FPLP cable is a plenum-rated cable. It is suitable for use in plenums, ducts, and other similar environmental air spaces. FPLP cables are fire resistant and in the event of a fire produce minimal smoke.

FPLR cables are rated for use in riser installations. This cable can be run vertically from floor to floor because it has a fire rating that prevents the fire from spreading from floor to floor. These types of cables prevent the fire from spreading into other floors of the building.

FPL (Non-Plenum) cable is non-plenum rated fire alarm cable. As per the NEC®, FPL type cable is suitable for general purpose fire alarm use. Unless installed in an approved raceway, type FPL cable it is not suitable for installation in risers, ducts, plenums, or other spaces used for environmental air. FPL cables resist the spread of fire.

The NEC® allows cable substitution (using type FPLP in lieu of FPLR) if a specified order is followed. Typically, type FPLP cable can be used in any location where FPLR is required, but not vice versa. Type FPLR can be used in any installation where FPL is required but not vice versa.

Under certain installation, a design engineer may call for the installation of CI cables. Circuit integrity (CI) cable is usually soft-jacketed with solid conductors and is listed for use in fire alarm and emergency voice communications systems. The cable's soft and flexible insulating material changes state when exposed to high temperature conditions, creating a fire resistant insulator to protect the conductors. When other codes and standards (Building Codes, NFPA 72®, NFPA 101®) require that wiring or cables have a 2-hour fire rating, CI cables can be used to comply with these requirements. NEC® 760.24(B) requires that Circuit integrity (CI) cables be supported at a distance not exceeding 24 in. Cable supports and fasteners shall be steel. In addition, strict mounting and installation requirements from the manufacturer shall be followed.

QUESTIONS

1. Portions of old, abandoned fire alarm cables must be _____, according to the NEC®.
   a. Red in color.
   b. Removed.
   c. Re-installed.
   d. Accessible.

2. Circuit conductors that extend from the circuit breaker to the terminals on the fire alarm control unit are known as _____.
   a. Non-power limited fire alarm conductors.
   b. Power-limited fire alarm conductors.
   c. Low voltage fire alarm conductors.
   d. High-voltage fire alarm conductors.

3. Circuit conductors that connect the (24VDC) horns and strobes to the initiating device circuit terminals on the fire alarm control unit are known as _____.
   a. Non-power limited fire alarm conductors.
   b. Power-limited fire alarm conductors.
   c. Low voltage fire alarm conductors.
   d. High-voltage fire alarm conductors.

4. When fire alarm cables are used for future use, they shall be _____.
   a. Red in color.
   b. Removed.
   c. Identified with a tag.
   d. Identified with a green color.

5. Fire alarm cables installed to connect to a heat detector at the top of the elevator shaft shall be _____.
   a. Installed in an approved raceway.
   b. Rated for plenum installations.
   c. Not greater than 3 feet in length.
   d. Installed exposed as close as possible to the walls of the shaft.

6. Under which of the following conditions can fire alarm cables be supported to a conduit?
   a. If the straps used to support the cables are fire rated.
   b. If the conduit is minimum of 2 inches.
   c. If the cable is riser rated.
   d. Under no condition.

7. Which type of cable designation can be used for going from one floor to another?
   a. FPLP
   b. FPLR
   c. FPL
   d. A and B only.

8. The circuit conductors that supply power to the fire alarm system shall be

   _____.
   a. Minimum #18 AWG
   b. Minimum #10 AWG
   c. Copper only.
   d. Aluminum only.

9. A fused disconnect switch was installed to supply power to a fire alarm system. The disconnect switch shall be _____.
   a. Painted red and identified as per the load served.
   b. Installed adjacent to the fire alarm control unit.
   c. Installed with 25 feet of the fire alarm control unit.
   d. Marked with a horse power rating.

10. FPL type cable is suitable for _____.
    a. Floor to floor installations.
    b. Plenums and duct work.
    c. Connecting to a smoke detector on the same room as the fire alarm control unit.
    d. Both A and B.

Chapter 5

OBJECTIVES:

➤ Describe symbols listed on the fire alarm plans.

➤ Describe the riser diagram and its use.

➤ Use fire alarm floor plans to describe the layout of fire alarm devices.

➤ Understand the use of the matrix of operations.

Fire Alarm Plans and Symbols

Fire alarm plans are, under most situations, developed by an engineering firm experienced in the design of fire alarm systems. The designer will use computer aided design software to develop the plans. The current software of choice by most designers is AutoCAD®. A designer will either use existing computer drawings of the floor plans of the premises or they will need to survey the premises to create new floor plans. The designer will then use his/her software of choice to "drag and drop" symbols, create notes, generate the matrix of operations and connect devices to finalize the plans. After the plans have gone through several reviews, they are generally submitted to the authority having jurisdiction for an official review. The AHJ will review the plans to make sure they comply with applicable codes and standards. Upon acceptance by the AHJ, the plans can then be executed by the installer.

Though many jurisdictions require plans be approved prior to beginning of work, this isn't always followed. In a rush to get a building or project completed, many installers begin running cabling and installing devices while plans are still being reviewed by the AHJ. Though many times this will save money and time for the building owners, a serious conflict can occur if the wrong system is installed. For example, a designer originally designs a system without voice communication, and the system is partially installed. However, the AHJ, upon review of the plans, requires that the system include voice communication. As a result, modification to the system design will cause time and money lost for everyone involved.

Fire Alarm Symbols

Symbols on a fire alarm plan generally depends on the engineering company used to develop the plans. Many engineering firms adhere to the symbols listed on NFPA 170®: Standard for Fire Safety and Emergency Symbols. Other engineering firms use symbols they created themselves. Either way, a symbols legend should exist on the plans to allow the installer to identify the devices.

Fire alarm plans will also include notes listed by the designer. These notes can include certain height requirements for devices, mounting procedures to follow, as well as fire rating on certain cables. Installers should take the time to read notes on the plans to make sure they are following the engineering design intended by the designer. Figure 73 is a symbols list from an actual engineering firm. This firm uses a polygon with a capital D letter to symbolize a duct detector, or an air-duct smoke detector. The S and R denotes that the duct detector will either be installed on the return side of the duct work or supply side of the duct work respectively.

A polygon with the letter H denotes a heat detector while the same figure but with an S denotes a smoke detector. Generally, the latter represents a spot-type smoke detector rather than any other smoke detector such as a projected beam.

A square with the letters SL denotes a visible notification appliance, or a strobe only. A visual and audible notification appliance, horn/strobe, is denoted by a square and a triangle with the letters H/S. These plans show an addressable pull station as the letters PS with a square. Note that the plans are calling for an addressable pull station rather than a conventional pull station.

The fire alarm control panel is denoted with the letters FACP within a rectangle. Note that generally, the fire alarm control panel and fire alarm control unit are the same. A water flow monitoring switch is a rectangle with the letter F inside; F representing "Flow", while a square with a TS represents a tamper switch; which is accomplished using a supervisory initiating-device sprinkler control valve monitoring switch. It shall be noted that the engineer or designer has specified, to the fire alarm installer, that both the water flow and tamper switch shall be furnished by others. These two devices are generally furnished by the sprinkler contractor, or the plumber or steam-fitter. The plumber drills the hole on the sprinkler piping and mounts the water flow device. The fire alarm installer then makes the final wiring connections and programming of the devices. Many times the fire alarm installation is delayed or behind schedule due to the numerous trades that are involved in the interconnection of the fire alarm system.

FIGURE 73

Monitoring modules, which allow an addressable fire alarm system to monitor open/close (normal/off-normal) conditions on conventional equipment, is denoted as an M inside a polygon. A remote annunciator is a square with the letters ANN inside. Many other engineers or designers will use RA instead of ANN. An audible notification appliance is similar to the horn/strobe but with only the letter H. Air handling units are generally shut-down using dry-contact relays, which allows low voltage to "control" higher voltages. This fan shut down relay is listed as the letters F/S within a rectangle.

If the fire alarm installer always works with the same designer or engineering firm, it is usually the case that the same symbols will be used.

Riser Diagram

The riser diagram shows all fire alarm equipment on a one-line style diagram. Figure 74 is a riser diagram that allows the installer to determine the amount of NAC circuits that the designer requires as well as the zones or data loops. The riser diagram is unlike a floor plan, as it will not show the location on the premises where the devices are to be installed.

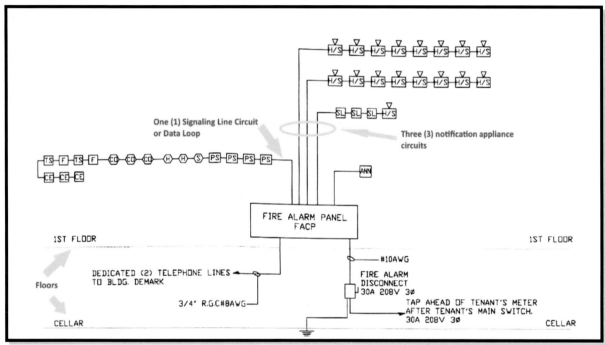

FIGURE 74

Figure 74 shows a riser diagram of a fire alarm system protecting a day care. The diagram shows that the installer is to provide three separate notification appliance circuits as well as one data loop or one SLC circuit. The riser must clearly identify the floor where the fire alarm control unit will be installed as well as where the disconnect means will be located. The number of devices (smoke detectors, strobes, horns, etc.) shown on the riser diagram must match the number of devices on the floor plans.

It is very common for field changes to occur after the design has been finalized. For example, a change in the layout of a building may prompt additional devices such as smoke detectors or notification appliances. When these changes occur, the record drawings must be updated to reflect such changes. As-built drawings are created at the end of a fire alarm installation to reflect the final installation including any added or removed devices. At the completion of the

Installation, these as-built drawings must be delivered to the owner of the system. Usually, the as-built drawings are framed adjacent to the fire alarm control unit.

Fire Alarm System Floor Plans

The fire alarm system floor plans will layout the location of the fire alarm devices. The floor plans are basically a "bird's eye view" of the space or premises where the fire alarm system and its devices are to be installed. Generally, unless notes are added, the floor plans will not show elevation requirements for the devices. A fire alarm installer will have to use NFPA 72® and other applicable code requirements to determine if a device should be installed where it is displayed on the floor plans. For example, floor plans show a strobe to be installed on a particular wall of a bathroom, but field changes have called for a utility closet to be installed on that wall. The installer would then have to make the decision to install the device on a different wall within the bathroom. In short, floor plans are usually created before the structure is built, which means that changes can and will occur. An installer has to use his judgement and experience in working with these changes. In addition, communication between the installer and designer or engineer is very critical as information from the field can be shared to the design engineer so that he/she can make the necessary changes.

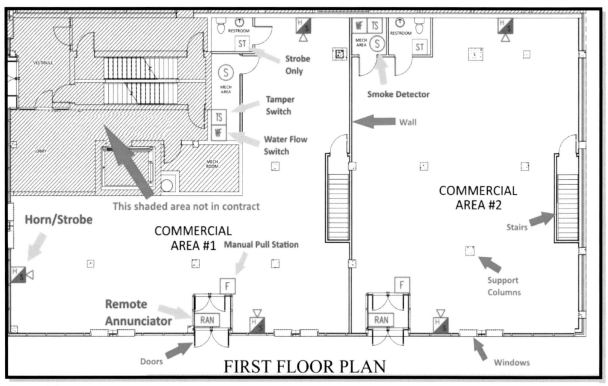

FIGURE 75

Figure 75 is a floor plan of a fire alarm system installed in a commercial space. The figure shows how the devices are laid out. Again, the installer's job is to read and interpret the symbols, and install the devices in the designed spaces.

A designer should always label the use of each room on the floor plans. Whether the room is an electrical room, mechanical room, employee lounge area or bathroom. The symbols used by the designer or engineer in figure 75 differ from those we previously looked at. As was specified earlier, different design firms use different symbols. Figure 77 shows an area that is shaded, which means that this area is not in contract, no fire alarm devices will be installed in this area. This is usually because the shaded area is either protected by another fire alarm system, or it isn't required by building code (or other applicable code) to be protected by a fire alarm system.

Figure 77 is of the same fire alarm system floor plans but of the cellar level.

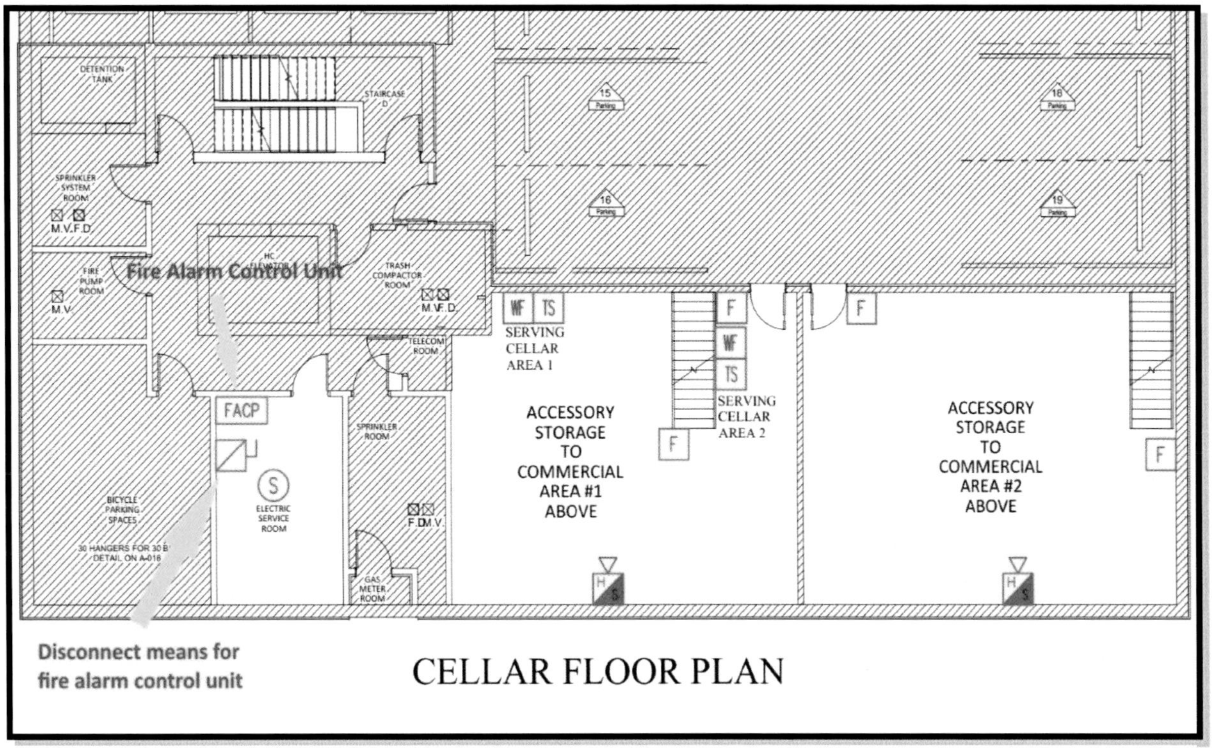

FIGURE 77

As per the floor plans, the fire alarm control unit will be installed in the electrical service room in the cellar. In addition, the fire alarm disconnect means is also to be installed in the same room as the fire alarm control unit.

Figure 78 shows a floor plan of a fire alarm system installed in a low-rise hotel. Building codes within the jurisdiction of the hotel mandates that smoke detection and carbon monoxide detection be provided for hotel guest rooms. Also, fire smoke dampers are denoted with the letters FSD. Because these fire smoke dampers are usually high voltage (120VAC), a high-voltage relay must be used to close the louvers.

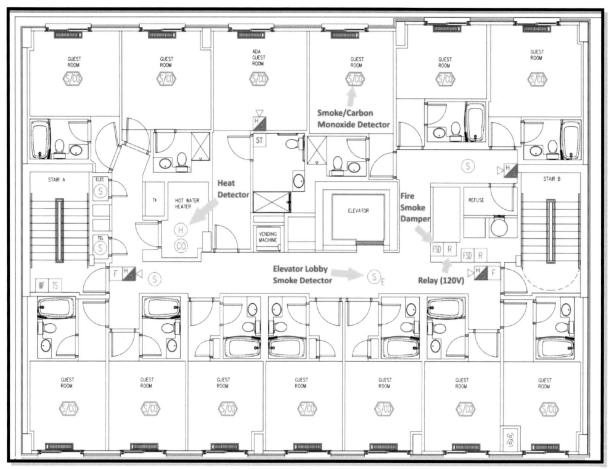

FIGURE 78

Fire Alarm Matrix of Operation (Input/Output)

The floor plans and riser diagram offer the installer information as to where devices are located and the amount of circuits to run. The functionality of the fire alarm system is determined by the matrix of operation or "input/output" matrix. As was discussed earlier, inputs are initiating devices. They "send" an input signal to the fire alarm control unit. The fire alarm control unit will activate certain outputs, as was programmed by the installer based off the matrix. Examples of outputs are activation of the horns and strobes, releasing of electrically held doors, shutting down supply fans, recalling the elevator or transmitting a signal to a central monitoring station.

Once the fire alarm system has been installed, programming can begin. The programmer or installer will use the matrix of operation to determine which outputs to activate once an input has been received. Figure 79 is a matrix of operation for a fire alarm system installed in a hotel. The inputs are listed as rows, while the outputs are shown as columns. To determine which output is activated after a certain input is received, we simply read through the row of the input and apply the outputs corresponding to that row that have a checked mark. For example, according to the matrix of operation, activation of a smoke detector will activate the following outputs: activate alarm horns with temporal 3 code, activate strobes throughout the space, activate display and audible signal at panel and remote annunciator, transmit an alarm signal to central office, shut down fans over 2000 CFM and activate fire smoke dampers. An input from a tamper switch will activate the following outputs: activate display and audible signal at the panel and remote annunciator and transmit a trouble signal to central station.

FIRE ALARM MATRIX

INPUT \ OUTPUT	ACTIVATE ALARM HORNS WITH TEMPORAL 3 CODE	ACTIVATE STROBES THROUGHOUT THE SPACE	ACTIVATE DISPLAY AND AUDIBLE SIGNAL AT PANEL AND REMOTE ANNUNCIATOR	ALARM SIGNAL TO CENTRAL OFFICE	SUPERVISORY SIGNAL TO CENTRAL OFFICE	TROUBLE SIGNAL TO CENTRAL OFFICE	CO SIGNAL TO CENTRAL STATION	SHUT DOWN FANS OVER 2000 CFM	ACTIVATE SMOKE/CO DETECTOR SOUNDER BASE	ACTIVATION OF FIRE SMOKE DAMPERS	ACTIVATE ELEVATOR RECALL
MANUAL PULL STATION	✓	✓	✓	✓						✓	
SMOKE DETECTOR	✓	✓	✓	✓				✓		✓	
ELEVATOR SMOKE DETECTOR	✓	✓	✓	✓				✓		✓	✓
CARBON MONOXIDE DETECTOR			✓			✓	✓		✓		
DUCT SMOKE DETECTOR	✓	✓	✓	✓				✓		✓	
WATERFLOW SWITCH	✓	✓	✓	✓				✓		✓	✓
TAMPER SWITCH			✓			✓					
HEAT DETECTOR	✓	✓	✓	✓				✓		✓	
GUEST ROOM SMOKE DETECTOR (SEE NOTE 1)			✓		✓				✓		
GUEST ROOM CO DETECTOR			✓		✓		✓		✓		
FAILURE OF SYSTEM AND COMPONENTS			✓			✓					
FIRE PUMP (RUN, FAIL, PHASE REVERSAL)			✓		✓						
GENERATOR (RUN, FAIL)			✓		✓						

FIGURE 79

The matrix of operation also shows that the fire alarm system is to "monitor" conditions on the fire pump and generator. Many jurisdictions require that when a fire alarm system is provided with emergency secondary power (generator), run and fail conditions of that generator shall be monitored by the fire alarm system. As discussed earlier, monitoring can be accomplished using monitoring modules. The fire alarm installer works in conjunction with the generator supplier or installer to determine which terminals on the generator control equipment the monitoring module will be connected to.

Fire pump run, fail and phase reversal will activate the same outputs, as per the matrix of operation. Only two inputs will cause the elevator to recall, that is activation of an elevator smoke detector or a water flow switch. This input-output correlation changes from jurisdiction to jurisdiction. Other jurisdictions require that any alarm condition (manual pull station, duct smoke detector) shall cause the elevator to recall.

Programming of these input-output correlations, as discussed earlier, depends on the fire alarm system used. Many systems use software that enables the programmer to associate an input with an output by simply using a graphic user interface with drop down options; others are a bit more complicated, requiring the programmer to use Boolean algebra to establish rules.

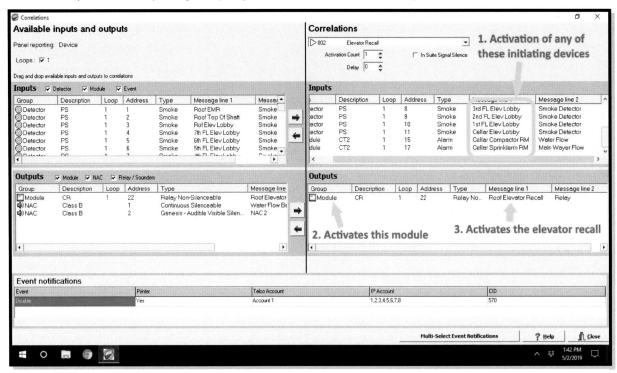

FIGURE 80

Figure 80 is a screenshot of a programming window for a fire alarm system installed in a residential building. Programming of the inputs and outputs is done through a graphic user interphase. Input devices are given a description by the programmer and are associated or correlated with an output. The figure shows that according to the programming, activation of any of the initiating devices selected will activate a module with output address 22, which will activate the elevator recall.

After the programming of the devices have been completed on the computer, the programmer must then save the settings and update the syntax or functionality on the firmware of the fire alarm control unit. This is accomplished by physically connecting the computer to the fire alarm control unit using a USB cable, serial or parallel cable or by any other means required by the manufacturer. Some systems can also be updated remotely by a technician; however, many jurisdictions prohibit such practice since the changes cannot be tested if the technician is not at the premises.

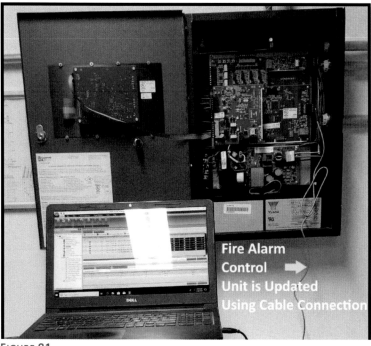

Other systems allow basic programming to be done using the buttons and display on the fire alarm control unit itself, meaning no computer is required. These systems are very limited however, and take up a lot of time to create input and output rules. After changes are completed and the firmware on the fire alarm control unit has been updated, the technician should test the changes to make sure that no other outputs were inadvertently affected.

FIGURE 81

QUESTIONS

1. _____ provides standard symbols used to communicate fire safety, emergency, and associated hazards information.
   a. NEC®
   b. NFPA 170®
   c. NFPA 72®
   d. NFPA 70®

2. Who must receive and keep the as built drawings of a fire alarm system?
   a. AHJ
   b. Owner of the system
   c. Fire Department
   d. None of the above

3. According to the fire alarm system symbol list in this chapter, A polygon with the letter H denotes a _____.
   a. Smoke Detector
   b. High Pressure Switch
   c. Heat Detector
   d. None of the above

4. Is the following statement true or false? A riser diagram allows the installer to determine the amount of NAC circuits that the designer requires.
   a. True
   b. False

5. _____ is a computer-aided drafting software program used to create blueprints for buildings and design fire alarm floor plans.
   a. MS Word
   b. Windows
   c. AutoCAD
   d. Linux

6. Is the following statement true or false? The fire alarm floor plans will layout the location of the fire alarm devices.
   a. False
   b. True

7. If the fire pump run activates, which of the following outputs activate?
   a. All strobes activate
   b. Activates display and audible signal at FACP and remote annunciator
   c. Sends supervisory signal to central station
   d. Only answers A & C
   e. Only answers B & C

8. The functionality (input/output) of the fire alarm system is determined by _____?
   a. The floor plans
   b. Riser diagram
   c. Matrix of operation
   d. None of the above

9. Is the following statement true or false? The matrix of operation indicates to the programmers, which outputs activate once an input has been received.
   a. True
   b. False

10. Is the following statement true or false? AutoCAD is software that many designers use to develop fire alarm plans.
    a. False
    b. True

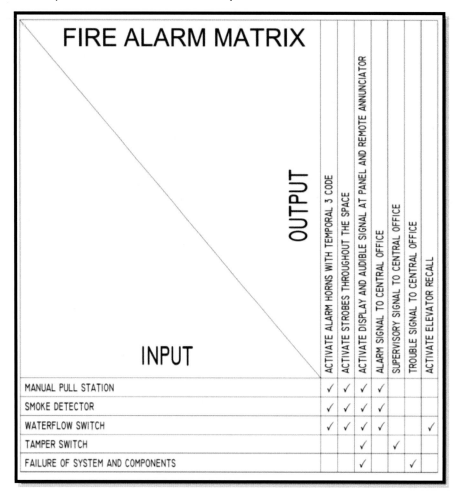

11. According to the matrix operation, if a manual pull station activates, which of the following outputs activate?
    a. Horns activate with temporal 3 code
    b. All strobes activate
    c. Elevator(s) recall(s)
    d. All of the above
    e. Only answers A & B

12. According to the matrix operation, if a water flow switch activates, which of the following outputs activate?
    a. Horns activate with temporal 3 code
    b. All strobes activate
    c. Elevator(s) recall(s)
    d. All of the above

13. According to the matrix operation, activation of which input would result in the fire alarm control unit transmitting a trouble signal to Central Office?
    a. An open notification appliances circuit
    b. Smoke detector
    c. Manual pull station
    d. All of the above
    e. Only answer A & C

14. According to the matrix of operation, activation of a sprinkler control valve will result in which output(s) activating?
    a. An audible signal at the fire alarm control unit
    b. An audible signal at the remote annunciator
    c. A supervisory signal to Central Office
    d. All of the above
    e. None of the above

15. Activation of which inputs will result in the activation of the horns/strobes?
    a. Tamper Switch
    b. Pull Station
    c. Smoke Detector
    d. Water Flow Switch
    e. b, c and d only

Use the following matrix of operations for questions 16-20.

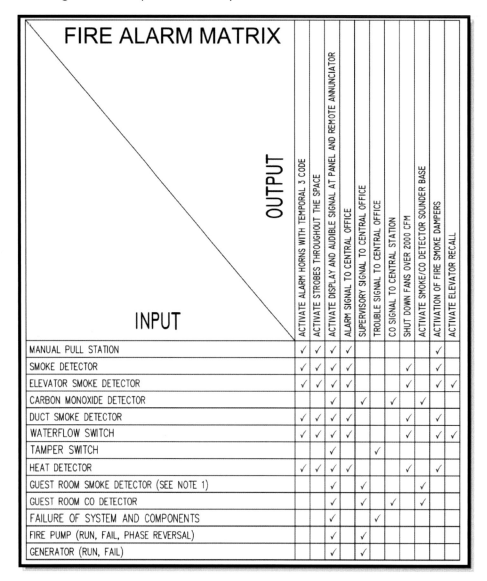

FIRE ALARM MATRIX

INPUT \ OUTPUT	ACTIVATE ALARM HORNS WITH TEMPORAL 3 CODE	ACTIVATE STROBES THROUGHOUT THE SPACE	ACTIVATE DISPLAY AND AUDIBLE SIGNAL AT PANEL AND REMOTE ANNUNCIATOR	ALARM SIGNAL TO CENTRAL OFFICE	SUPERVISORY SIGNAL TO CENTRAL OFFICE	TROUBLE SIGNAL TO CENTRAL OFFICE	CO SIGNAL TO CENTRAL STATION	SHUT DOWN FANS OVER 2000 CFM	ACTIVATE SMOKE/CO DETECTOR SOUNDER BASE	ACTIVATION OF FIRE SMOKE DAMPERS	ACTIVATE ELEVATOR RECALL
MANUAL PULL STATION	✓	✓	✓	✓						✓	
SMOKE DETECTOR	✓	✓	✓	✓					✓	✓	
ELEVATOR SMOKE DETECTOR	✓	✓	✓	✓					✓	✓	✓
CARBON MONOXIDE DETECTOR		✓					✓		✓		
DUCT SMOKE DETECTOR	✓	✓	✓	✓					✓	✓	
WATERFLOW SWITCH	✓	✓	✓	✓					✓	✓	✓
TAMPER SWITCH		✓				✓					
HEAT DETECTOR	✓	✓	✓	✓					✓	✓	
GUEST ROOM SMOKE DETECTOR (SEE NOTE 1)		✓			✓				✓		
GUEST ROOM CO DETECTOR		✓			✓			✓	✓		
FAILURE OF SYSTEM AND COMPONENTS			✓			✓					
FIRE PUMP (RUN, FAIL, PHASE REVERSAL)			✓		✓						
GENERATOR (RUN, FAIL)			✓		✓						

16. According to the matrix operation, if the generator on the roof is powered on, the fire alarm control unit will activate which output?
    a. Horns activate with temporal 3 code
    b. Activates display and audible signal at FACP and remote annunciator
    c. Supervisory signal to central station
    d. None of the above
    e. Only answers B and C

17. According to the matrix operation, if a carbon monoxide detector activates, which of the following outputs activate?
    a. Activate smoke/CO detector sounder base
    b. Activates display and audible signal at FACP and remote annunciator
    c. Supervisory signal to central station
    d. All of above answers
    e. Only answers A & B

18. True or False. According to the matrix of operation, activation of a manual pull station will recall the building elevators to the designated level?
    a. True
    b. False

19. According to the matrix operation, if a guest room smoke detector activates, which of the following outputs activate?
    a. Activates display and audible signal at FACP and remote annunciator
    b. Activate smoke/CO detector sounder base
    c. Supervisory signal to central station
    d. All of the above answers
    e. Only answers A & B

20. According to the matrix of operation, activation of which input will shut-down any building fan over 2000 CFM?
    a. Any smoke detector
    b. Heat detector
    c. Water flow
    d. All of the above
    e. None of the above

The fire alarm field is one with lots of growth. A fire alarm company employee can start as an inspector of existing installations, conducting the yearly inspections on the systems; move up to installer; then programmer and eventually designer of the system. To climb each of the steps mentioned above doesn't require college degrees, but rather the determination and dedication by you, the future fire alarm technician.

Experience is sometimes not enough to show your worth to a company. That is why becoming certified by a third party is crucial for growing within the fire alarm industry. One certification in fire alarms that is widely accepted and recognized is NICET®. NICET® stands for the National Institute of Certification of Engineering Technologies®. NICET® offers 2 certifications for the fire alarm industry:

- Fire Alarm Systems Certification – 4 Levels
- Inspection & Testing of Fire Alarm Systems Certification – 2 Levels

For most companies, being NICET® certified means that your expertise and knowledge have been evaluated and tested by an objective third party. Many jurisdictions require that any person installing or testing fire alarm equipment hold a NICET® certification. Your goal, once you begin working in the exciting field of fire alarms, should be to achieve the highest level of NICET® certification. NFPA 72® 10.5.2 specifies that fire alarm systems and emergency communications systems installation personnel shall be qualified or shall be supervised by persons who are qualified in the installation, inspection, and testing of the systems. Nationally recognized fire alarm certification programs might include those programs offered by the International Municipal Signal Association® (IMSA), National Institute for Certification in Engineering Technologies® (NICET), and the Electronic Security Association (ESA).

Requirements to become a NICET® certified fire alarm technician include submitting work experience to meet the minimum level for each level the applicant wishes to apply. In addition, the applicant must pass a computer based exam administered at a testing center. Upon completion, the technician will receive a card identifying his/her level of certification.

Once the technician is certified they must renew their application every 3 years. A certified technician must complete continuing education courses or credits to maintain his/her level of certification. Credits are obtained by attending classroom sessions or completing online based courses. Keep in mind that all courses completed must be relevant to fire alarm systems. Usually, the employer will aid in providing training to their certified technician. Technicians can be trained by fire alarm system vendors, such as Siemens or Edwards, in programming aspects. This particular type of training qualifies as maintaining credits for the certification.

Becoming certified should be at the very top of any fire alarm technician's list. I wish you the best in your new journey in becoming a fire alarm technician.

Made in the USA
Columbia, SC
20 November 2020